COOKED IN A FLASH

Jenny BRISTOW

APPLETREE PRESS

First published in 1998 by
The Appletree Press Ltd
The Old Potato Station
14 Howard Street South
Belfast BT7 1AP
Tel: +44 (0) 28 90 243074
Fax:+44 (0) 28 90 246756
E-mail:reception@appletree.ie
Web Site:www.irelandseye.ie

Cooked in a Flash

A catalogue record for this book
is available from The British Library.

ISBN 0-86281-742-0

10 9 8 7 6 5 4

CONTENTS

Introduction

Cooked in a Flash is about recipes and food ideas for everyone, which do not take all day to make. It is food for people like myself who enjoy cooking and prefer to eat at home but don't have hours to spend in the kitchen each day. We cook to feed hungry and often demanding people, usually with little notice or time to plan. These recipes address the demands of modern, hectic living.

It is amazing how food has changed over the last few years. We are busier with less time to shop or spend at home. The need for good, healthy food remains but our busy lifestyles dismiss the traditional meat and two vegetables. We require speedy snacks, food that's fat free and fast to prepare. Lunches that are prepared in a flash are the order of the day. Yet there is no compromise on flavour, goodness or presentation. The quicker food cooks, often the better it tastes.

I know you will be delighted with the shorter preparation and cooking times, making it possible to have a meal on the table in less than the time it takes to heat a ready-made meal.

I make no apology for using ready-made breads and supermarket products, and turning these into speedy snacks such as floury baps with melting cheese and poached fruit, or ciabatta layered with pickles, salad and steak slices adding a new meaning to a *minute* steak.

As in previous books, I am sure you will find food ideas for everyone - a fresh way with ham roasted in a Mediterranean manner and crusted for a stunning centre piece, quickly-cooked lamb cutlets topped with black olive paste for an Italian rack of lamb, ideal for dinner in a dash. If you want good food that cooks quickly, a bacon, brie and filo tart might be just what you need. Whatever your lifestyle, I hope you will find many new recipes here for you to prepare and enjoy.

Acknowledgements

I would like to acknowledge the assistance of the following people and organisations in both the making of the television series and the writing of the accompanying book.

With thanks to:
Ruth Johnston, Producer, Director and friend who kept me motivated and tried so hard to prevent me from being a late sort of person. Alan Bremner, Controller of Programming, for the interest in contemporary cuisine. Mike McCann, Head of Public Affairs, for his encouragement and humour in the co-ordinating of this book with the series *Cooked in a Flash*.

The UTV team: Sam Christie, Ronnie Martin, Bill Rowan, Malachy Marken, Mary McCleave and Ken McNally.

The photography team: Robert McKeag, Howard Ward and Food Stylist Ann Bryan.

The team at Appletree Press for their support and advice throughout this book: John Murphy, publisher; Catherine McIlvenna, editor; Robert Blackwell, Jim Black and Claire Skillen.

Maureen Best and Sally Stirling for their help behind the scenes, in the kitchen and in helping to source the most amazing fruit, vegetables and food at its very best. Vera McCready for typing this text, often at weekends and late at night. David Flynn of Marlborough Antiques, Belfast, who just could not have been more helpful. Nicholas Mosse Pottery, Kilkenny; Christine Foy, Mullaghmeen Pottery, Enniskillen; Michelle Kershaw at Lakeland Plastics; Habitat, Belfast; Peter Nicholl at La Cucina Cookshops; Debenhams, Belfast; Sally Backus, Ballymena for the fresh flower arrangements; Moores of Coleraine; Catherine McMillan, Beechgrove Interiors, Ballymena; John Cameron at Cameron's, Ballymena; Ken Crockett at Balmoral Flowers; Ian McKay and Maud Hamill at Calor Gas; D J Lockhart at Platinum Homewares; Lagostina Cuisine Cookware; Le Creuset; John Newell at Kenwood; Linda Stewart at the Craft Stop, Cullybackey.

Jenny Bristow

Conversion of Measurements

The following equivalents were used in converting between metric and imperial measurements.

Temperature

Temp°C	Temp°F	Gas Mark
110	225	¼
120	250	½
140	275	1
150	300	2
160	325	3
180	350	4
190	375	5
200	400	6
220	425	7
230	450	8
240	475	9

Volume

Vol ml/L	Vol Pt/ fl oz
3.40L	6pt
2.75L	5pt
2.25L	4pt
1.7L	3pt
1.4L	2½pt
1.1L	2pt
850ml	1½pt
570ml	1pt
425ml	¾pt
380ml	⅔pt
280ml	½pt
200ml	7fl oz
170ml	6fl oz
140ml	¼pt
115ml	4fl oz
70ml	⅛pt

Weight

Weight Kg	Weight lb
1.35kg	3lb
900g	2lb
680g	1½ lb
450g	1lb
400g	14oz
340g	12oz
285g	10oz
225g	8oz
200g	7oz
170g	6oz
140g	5oz
115g	4oz
85g	3oz
70g	2½oz
55g	2oz
45g	1½oz
30g	1oz
15g	½oz

Surfing The
WEEKEND

———◆◆◆———

The weekend is a very special part of the week that most people enjoy. However, it's also the time when extra demands are made on the cook in charge to provide meals for every occasion.

There is no better way to enjoy a weekend than with good food. A combination of breakfasts that are simple to make, relaxed lunches served in a bowl, well behaved puddings and main courses brimming with flavour and goodness – now, that's surfing the weekend.

A HEALTHY SUNSHINE BREAKFAST

For those who prefer a robust breakfast, this tasty potato galette made with grated potato and a fine batter then fried in a pan in hot foamy butter is perfect. ·

2 large potatoes, grated
2 tsp plain flour
1/2 tsp salt
1 tsp baking powder
milk to mix to a smooth batter

15g/1/2oz butter
1 dsp olive oil
100g/4oz sour cream
1 dsp chives
4-6 rashers of bacon

Serves 2

Peel and grate the potatoes, then squeeze from them as much water as possible. Add to a bowl and mix with the flour, salt, baking powder and milk. Mix to form a smooth batter, then cook in hot foaming butter and olive oil in individual-sized pancakes. Cook for two minutes on each side and drain on kitchen paper. Serve hot topped with sour cream, chives and crispy bacon.

A SUNSHINE FRUIT BOWL TOPPED WITH YOGHURT

For those who prefer a more fruity breakfast then dried fruits poached in orange juice are excellent, especially if lightly scented with cinnamon and cloves.

Orange Syrup
280ml/1/2pt orange juice
55g/2oz caster sugar
1 cinnamon stick
8 cloves

peel of 1/2 orange
1 packet 400g/1lb dried fruits
2-3 dsp yoghurt

Serves 6

Make the syrup by boiling together for 2 minutes the orange juice, sugar, spices and peel until dissolved. Add the dried fruits and poach gently for 25 minutes until the fruits have absorbed the liquids and become plump. Serve either warm or chilled topped with yoghurt.

NUTMEG FLAVOURED TURNIP

Here is a new treatment for an old-fashioned vegetable – the turnip or swede. In this recipe the turnip is livened up with a hint of nutmeg and baked in the oven.

1 turnip, cut into fine slices
1 tsp nutmeg
425ml/3/4 pint milk
140ml/1/4pt cream

1 onion, finely chopped
1 clove garlic
salt and pepper

Serves 6

Cut the turnip into fine slices, arrange in a serving dish and sprinkle with nutmeg.
In a saucepan heat together the milk and cream. Add the onion, garlic, salt and pepper. Bring to

the boil then turn off the heat and leave to infuse for 10 minutes before pouring over the turnip and baking in the oven at 375°F/190°C/gas number 5 for 1 hour approximately.

PARSLEY AND POLENTA BREAD

Polenta, to give it its Italian name, is a golden maize meal we have known for years, which has become very popular in bread. With its canary yellow colour and robust texture of grainy sand, it makes an interesting bread.

115g/4oz polenta
115g/4oz self-raising flour
2 tsp baking powder
1 tsp salt
2 dsp parsley, chopped

280ml/½ pint water
55g/2oz butter
280ml/½ pint milk
3 eggs, lightly beaten

Serves 8

Mix together in a large bowl the polenta, self-raising flour, baking powder and salt. Add the parsley and mix well together. Heat the water, add the butter and melt. When still warm, add to the flour. Mix quickly and add the milk and the lightly beaten egg to form a smooth batter. Pour into a greased, long tin and bake in the oven at 400°F/200°C/gas number 6 for 30 minutes.

WEEKEND RISOTTO OF WILD RICE, VEGETABLES & HONEY MARINATED DUCK

Here is a wonderful rice dish for the weekend that is equally as good at lunchtime as it is in the evening. This is a risotto type dish packed full of flavour with beans, lentils, vegetables and topped with duck breasts. This dish is ideal for the vegetarian when served without the duck breast.

2 dsp oil
1 onion, finel chopped
450g/1lb long grain rice
1.1L/2pt vegetable stock
115g/4oz wild rice
550ml/1pt stock
2 cloves garlic
225g/8oz sliced peppers

225g/8oz mushrooms, sliced
225g/8oz green lentils
115g/4oz sprouting beans (optional)
3 duck breasts
2 dsp oil
4 dsp honey
1" root ginger
black pepper

Serves 10

Heat 1 dsp oil in a large pan, gently fry the onion for several minutes, then add the long grain rice and toss around. Pour in the stock and simmer for 10-12 minutes until absorbed. In a seperate pan, cook the wild rice in boiling salted water for 25 minutes until cooked and tender, then mix the two rices together. Heat the oil, add the garlic and cook until nutty and golden. Add the peppers and mushrooms, cook for 3-4 minutes then add the cooked lentils and sprouting beans. Add to the rice and toss through. Skin the breasts then pour over a hot marinade of oil, honey and ginger. Grind with black pepper, cook on a grill pan for 2 minutes on either side and finish off in a hot oven at 425°F/220°C/gas number 7 for 6-7 minutes. Slice and serve over the top of the rice and vegetables tossed together.

Overleaf: parsley and polenta bread, weekend risotto of wild rice, vegetables and honey marinated duck

A WINTER WARMER OF A SPLIT PEA SOUP

Soup is one of the most versatile of foods, from the more delicate consommé to the more sturdy variety of heart-warming broth. I am using split peas to make a flavoursome winter-warming soup and like most soups it starts off with a good stock.

Ham Stock
1 ham shank, 900g/2lb approx.
3-4 litres/6pt water
1 carrot
1 stick celery
1 bay leaf
1 bunch parsley stalks
1 onion
1 potato

1 dsp oil
450g/1lb peas
1.7L/ 3pt ham stock
dash Tabasco
140ml/¼pt milk
Tabasco sauce
225g/8oz ham from shank

Serves 6-8

Make the stock by simmering together the ham shank, water, carrot, celery, bay leaf and parsley for 2-2½ hours to concentrate the flavour and reduce the liquid by half. Reduce any visible fat from the top then sieve. Sweat together the onion, potato and oil for 8-10 minutes until softened. Add the split peas, which have been steeped in cold water for at least 2 hours. Add the stock and simmer gently for 1¼ hours approximately until softened and tender. If preferred, the soup can be puréed. Add the milk, Tabasco and ham pieces from shank. Heat through and serve.

MY VERSION OF AN ULSTER FRY

Sunday morning is definitely the time for a relaxed breakfast. If you fancy a cooked one, then why not serve traditional bacon, tomatoes and mushrooms and spiced up scrambled eggs?

Spiced Scrambled Eggs
3 eggs
15g/½oz butter
2 dsp milk

1 dsp cottage cheese
½ tsp paprika pepper
few chives, chopped

TO SERVE: bacon, tomatoes, mushrooms

Serves 3

Beat the eggs lightly then add to the saucepan with the melted butter, milk, cottage cheese, paprika pepper, and chives. Cook for 2 minutes then serve hot with griddled bacon, tomatoes and mushrooms.

BLACKENED OLIVE OIL AND RED ONION CHAMP

Here's a change from the traditional champ made with scallions, milk and butter. The secret lies in the floury potatoes and a high temperature for the cooking of the onions to almost blacken them.

900g/2lb floury potatoes, cooked and mashed
1 dsp olive oil

1 red onion
1 dsp parsley, finely chopped

Serves 6

Boil and mash the potatoes and place in a serving dish. In a frying pan, heat the oil and add the red onion. Fry until blackened and crispy then sprinkle over the mashed potatoes. Garnish with finely chopped parsley.

A HONEY AND GINGER ROASTED CHICKEN

Chicken is one food that really can strut its stuff when it comes to cooking, regardless of whether you eat it 2-3 times a week. If you spatchcock it and leave it in an oriental marinade, you have a chicken which cooks in a shorter time and tastes delicious.

1 x 2.25kg/5lb chicken
4 dsp plum sauce
2 dsp honey
1 tsp whole-grain mustard

1" root ginger, finely chopped
1 tsp soy sauce
2 dsp olive oil
salt and pepper

Serves 8

Cut the chicken carefully down the back bone and open it out onto a foil-lined roasting dish. Make the marinade by mixing together the plum sauce, honey, mustard, ginger, soy sauce, olive oil and seasoning. Pour over the chicken then use a pastry brush to pat down well over the chicken. Roast the chicken in the oven at 375°F/190°C/ gas number 5 for approximately 1 1/2 - 2 hours until tender and cooked.

A LEMON AND SULTANA PUDDING

Proper puddings seem to have faded into the weekends because we are often far too busy during the week to make them. This intense, tangy flavoured, lemony pudding will separate out into two layers. Serve with yoghurt.

115g/4oz butter
225g/8oz sugar
4 lemons, rind and juice
4 egg yolks
155g/5oz self raising flour, sieved
280ml/1/2 pint milk

55g/2oz sultanas
70ml/1/8 pint sherry
4 egg whites, beaten stiffly
115g/4oz yoghurt
30g/1oz pistachio nuts, chopped

Serves 6

Cream the butter and sugar until soft. This mixture is difficult to cream due to the quantity of sugar. Add the lemon rind and egg yolks, and beat well. Add the sieved flour, lemon juice and milk in 2-3 additions. Mix well. Add the sultanas soaked in sherry then finally fold in the stiffly beaten egg whites. The folding in of the eggs is very important as this causes the lightness of the pudding. Cook in the oven at 375°F/190°C/ gas number 5 for 45 minutes. It is almost soufflé like and will rise up with the lemony saucy layer settling to the bottom. Serve with yoghurt lightly flavoured with chopped pistachio nuts.

Overleaf: lemon and sultana pudding

FEASTING IN A
FLASH

———◆━►✦◄━◆———

C ooking for feasts today is usually a relaxed
and casual affair, with most people preferring
less formal entertaining.

Can you think of a better way to celebrate those
special days in life other than feasting on good food? The
sort of food that looks stunning, tastes delicious and does
not take too long to cook.

A WARM AROMATIC COUSCOUS SALAD

Couscous is becoming almost as popular today as rice when you need an accompaniment to fish, chicken or meat. Yet it also makes an ideal main course dish for a party and here it can be served warm. The addition of well-flavoured stock and butter gives this dish such flavour.

850ml/1½pt chicken stock
450g/1lb couscous
2 stalks celery, sliced
6 spring onions, sliced
55g/2 oz butter, melted

225g/8oz apricots, sliced
225g/8oz sultanas
225g/8oz dates, chopped
55g/2oz pine nuts or hazelnuts
4 dsp parsley, finely chopped

Serves 8

Pour the warm stock over the couscous and leave to infuse for 12-15 minutes, until doubled in size and the liquid absorbed. In a small pan gently cook the celery and spring onions in the melted butter but do not brown. Add the sliced dried apricots, sultanas, dates, to celery and spring onions. Toss the salad into an ovenproof dish and warm in the oven at 375°F/190°C/gas number 5 for 12-15 minutes. Serve warm, sprinkled with pine nuts and finely chopped parsley.

POTATO SCALES

A very simple potato dish to go with whole baked salmon. The potatoes are very finely sliced and arranged in an ovenproof dish in layers until they resemble fish scales.

4-5 potatoes, finely sliced
280ml/½pt milk and cream, mixed
2 dsp chives, finely chopped
salt and pepper
1 egg, lightly beaten

Serves 6-8

Peel and slice the potatoes very finely and arrange in a well greased ovenproof dish. Pour over the milk and cream. Sprinkle with chives and season with salt and pepper. Brush with lightly beaten egg and bake in the oven at 425°F/220°C/gas number 8 for 45 minutes, until the milk has been absorbed and the potatoes are crispy and golden on top.

HAM COOKED THE MEDITERRANEAN WAY

Roasted in the oven with vegetables, herbs and wine, this is a very different way to serve ham. The sweet, spicy flavours of the Mediterranean are so tasty and this ham looks stunning as a centre piece for a buffet table.

1 unsmoked ham, 2.8-3.6kg/6-8lb
4.5L/6-8 pt cold water (to steep ham)
1 onion
2 stalks celery
1 bunch parsley
1 dsp dried oregano
1 dsp peppercorns
6-8 basil leaves
2 bay leaves, cracked

2 red peppers, sliced
2 yellow peppers, sliced
2 orange peppers, sliced
2 courgettes, sliced
1 aubergine, sliced
140 ml/¼pt white wine
55g/2oz demerara sugar
2 dsp honey

Serves 6

Soak the ham in cold water for 2-3 hours then place in a large pot with 6-8 pints of fresh, cold water. Add the onion, celery, parsley, dried oregano, peppercorns, basil and bay leaves. Bring to the boil and simmer for 1½-2 hours. Remove the ham from the pot of water and allow it to cool slightly before removing the rind and a layer of fat from the ham. Make a few casual scores over the top of the ham. Place the ham on a foil-lined roasting dish. Scatter the coarsely sliced vegetables around the ham. Pour over the wine, sugar and honey and bake in a hot oven at 400°F/200°C/gas number 6, for 45-60 minutes. Ham may require longer to cook so check before removing from oven. After cooking lift out the vegetables, spoon over the ham with juices as well and bake in the oven at 425°F/220°C/gas number 8 for 15-20 minutes, until vegetables are chargrilled and crispy. The vegetables can be studded to the ham to make it look more attractive.

AMARETTO AND STRAWBERRY CAKE

A very simple yet stunning cake made with bought biscuits and berries. This pudding does not hold and needs to be eaten within 1 hour of making. However, if fresh rather than frozen berries are used, this pudding will hold longer. Do not sweeten the fruit or it will weep in this pudding. Serve in a mould or individual glasses.

225g/8oz amaretto biscuits
115g/4oz yoghurt
115g/4oz fromage frais
450g/1lb fresh strawberries, raspberries and blueberries, mixed

TO DECORATE mint leaves, 30g/1oz icing sugar to decorate

Serves 6-8

Crush the biscuits and mix in a bowl with the yoghurt and fromage frais but be careful not to overmix. The addition of low fat cream cheese will help the pudding hold. Prepare the fruit. Cut the strawberries into slices but leave the raspberries and blueberries whole. Then mix with the broken amaretto biscuits mixture. Transfer to a lined 8" loose-bottomed tin. Chill in the fridge for 15-30 minutes. Unmould and decorate with fresh berries and mint leaves dusted with icing sugar.

Overleaf: amaretto and strawberry cake

A CHICKEN CASSEROLE WITH ROASTED CITRUS FRUITS

If you are cooking for a party, chicken is often a safe bet. Here is a tasty chicken casserole topped with citrus slices and almonds, flavoured with ginger and orange, which looks stunning and is light and tasty.

900g/2lb chicken fillets, cut into strips

Marinade
140ml/¼pt orange juice   *2 dsp balsamic vinegar*
70ml/⅛pt lime juice

1 dsp olive oil   *1 orange*
1" root ginger   *1 lemon*
1 bunch spring onions   *1 lime*
140ml/¼pt orange juice   *2 dsp honey*
140ml/¼pt chicken stock   *citrus slices*
2 dsp marmalade   *almonds, toasted*
2 dsp honey   *parsley, chopped*
salt and pepper

Serves 6

Place the chicken strips in a bowl. Make the marinade using the orange juice, lime juice and balsamic vinegar. Leave to sit for 10-15 minutes. In a large pan heat the oil and add the finely chopped root ginger. Cook until nutty brown then add the spring onion and cook. Drain the chicken from the marinade and add to the pan. Cook over a high heat to brown and caramelize the chicken. Add the remainder of the marinade, orange juice, stock and orange marmalade to thicken the sauce. Cut the fruits into fine slices, place on a baking sheet and brush with honey. Place below a hot grill or roast in the oven at 425°F/220°C/gas number 7 for 15-20 minutes. If cooking below the grill they should be cooked in 5-6 minutes.

Serve the casserole topped with citrus slices, toasted almonds and chopped parsley.

WHOLE BAKED SALMON

When it comes to a special occasion then you will find a whole salmon not only looks fabulous but also tastes delicious. For 8 people you will need a 4-5lb salmon. I find that baking it in the oven is one of the easiest and best ways to cook it. Clean it well and remember to cut out the gills as they cause a bitter aftertaste.

1 salmon, 2.3kg/4-5lb   *1 lemon, juice*
1 lemon   *140ml/¼pt white wine*
bunch parsley   *70ml/⅛pt stock, vegetable*
2 bay leaves   *55g/2oz butter*
salt and pepper

TO GARNISH 1 lemon, ½ cucumber, fresh fennel, dill and parsley

Serves 8

Place the prepared salmon onto a foil-lined baking sheet (double thickness). Fill the cavity of the fish with sliced lemon, parsley, bay leaves, salt and pepper. Pour over and around the fish the lemon juice, wine and a little stock. Cover the fish with butter then season and fold over the foil until it resembles a "tent". Leave it loose to allow the air to circulate. Cook in the oven at 425°F/220°C/gas number 7 for 6-7 minutes per lb. A 4-5lb salmon should take 35-40 minutes to cook. Allow to cool in the cooking liquid before removing from the foil. Remove the skin from the salmon and decorate with lemon, cucumber and herbs and serve cold.

ORANGE AND BITTER CHOCOLATE MERINGUE CAKE

Puddings for parties have to taste good, look great and it is a bonus if you can make some part of them in advance. The layered meringue can be made and stored in an airtight tin for 1-2 weeks. Do not make the layers of meringue too thick. The layers of filling are tasty and sharp in flavour with a variety of textures.

8 egg whites	115g/4oz hazelnuts, chopped and toasted
450g/1lb caster sugar	

Filling 1
225g/8oz bitter dark chocolate — 225g/8oz mascarpone cheese
2 dsp dark coffee

Filling 2
225g/8oz crème fraîche — ½ orange, rind only
1 orange, segmented and diced

Topping
225g/8oz kumquats — 55g/2oz caster sugar
½ orange, sliced and chopped — dash Cointreau
140ml/¼pt water — 2 dsp orange marmalade

TO DECORATE: chocolate leaves or caraque, sliced orange pieces

Serves 12

Beat the egg whites and half the sugar together until white and fluffy. Then lightly fold in the remainder of the sugar with a spatula and then the hazelnuts. Line three baking sheets with lightly greased, waxed paper. Draw a circle on the underneath side 9-10" diameter. Transfer to three lined baking sheets and cook in the oven at 275°F/140°C/gas number 1, for 1¼ hours. Cool and remove the paper from each layer. To make the fillings, melt the chocolate, add the coffee, then when almost cool mix with the mascarpone cheese. Beat well to form a smooth chocolate mousse. Set aside. Mix together the crème fraîche, orange slices and orange rind. Set aside. Poach the kumquats and sliced orange pieces in the sugar and water. Add the liqueur and orange marmalade and mix well. Use the fillings to layer the cake together and finish with a kumquat and marmalade layer on top. Decorate and serve with chocolate caraque and orange slices.

CUTTING THE FAT
AND BOOSTING THE
FLAVOUR

Today it is possible to create very tasty, low-fat versions of your everyday favourite meals, including roasts, pies and puddings.

The choice of fats and oils is vital to the flavour of many cooked dishes. Each has a different calorific value. There are some oils which are beneficial to our health, especially the monounsaturated olive oils.

Flavoured oils are one of the newest products on sale in supermarkets. Whichever one you use, the general advice is to reduce the oil and fat, and use only what you require, leaving scope for food flavours to come through in cooking.

ROASTED PORK CHOPS
WITH APPLES AND PLUMS

Pork today is bred to be leaner and in some cases, is lower in fat than lean beef. The method of cooking will also affect the fat content. That is why I find roasting an ideal way to develop the flavour, tenderise the meat and keep the fat in check.

4 loin pork chops, lean, with fat removed
2 dsp balsamic vinegar
225g/½lb baby onions, peeled
and cut into quarters
6-8 cloves
2 dsp honey
140ml/¼pt apple juice, unsweetened

4 eating apples, sliced
6-8 plums
30g/1oz demerara sugar
2 dsp redcurrant jelly
2 dsp parsley
4 potatoes, steamed

Serves 4

Place pork chops in a roasting dish. Pour over vinegar, onions, cloves, honey and apple juice. Place in a pre-heated oven at 450°F/230°C/gas number 8 for 5 minutes to seal the flavour. Reduce the heat to 375°F/190°C/gas number 5 when the chops go in. Cook for approximately 1 hour or until the pork is cooked to your satisfaction. Remove from the oven and add the sliced apples and plums dusted with demerara sugar. Return to oven and cook until the fruit has softened, approximately 15-20 minutes. Serve the pork chops and fruit on a serving dish. Bubble the meat juices and when boiling, thicken with redcurrant jelly. Spoon over the chops and garnish with parsley. Serve with steamed potatoes in their skins.

FILO CHICKEN PIE

It is possible to make a tasty chicken pie that is low fat provided you use filo pastry and do not brush with butter. Cook the filling in 1 tsp olive oil. Before slicing chicken into small pieces, trim off skin. Ensure the chicken pieces are finely sliced so that the chicken will cook quickly.

3-4 chicken fillets
2 dsp balsamic vinegar
salt and pepper
1 dsp olive oil
2 cloves garlic
1" root ginger
2-3 spring onions
1 red pepper, diced

1 green pepper, diced
1 yellow pepper, diced
115g/4oz bean sprouts
2 dsp soy sauce
2 carrots, finely sliced
2 dsp arrowroot and 1 dsp water, blended
6-8 sheets filo pastry
1 egg white

Serves 8-10

Remove the skin from the chicken fillets and cut into bite-sized pieces. Add the balsamic vinegar, salt and pepper, and toss. In a wok or large pan, heat 1 dsp olive oil. Add the marinated chicken pieces and cook for 3-4 minutes to seal the flavour. Add the garlic, ginger, spring onion, peppers, bean sprouts and carrot. Cook for 2-3 minutes. Season with 2 dsp soy sauce and thicken with 2 dsp of blended arrowroot. Cook for 1 minute and leave to cool. Brush the sheets of filo pastry with egg white mixed with olive oil. Layer 5-6 sheets into a round 8-9" diameter loose-bottomed tin. Spoon the cooked filling into the pastry case. Fold the overlapping layers of pastry over the top, brush with olive oil and egg white to glaze the top. Cook in the oven at 400°F/200°C/gas number 6 for 15-20 minutes until golden and crispy on top.

CREAMY WATERCRESS SOUP

This soup is quick and easy to make, low in fat and very tasty. It has a faint peppery flavour, is high in iron and is made with a low fat chicken stock. If sweating vegetables with such a small amount of oil, then leave the lid off the pan, stir often and add 2 dsp water to the oil.

1 tsp olive oil
4 potatoes, peeled and diced
4-5 spring onions, sliced
2 bags watercress, approx. 450g/1lb
1.1L/2pt chicken stock, skimmed and fat removed

salt and pepper
1 tsp lemon rind
1 dsp yoghurt

Serves 6

Heat the oil in the pan. Add the diced potato and sweat for 4-5 minutes. If the potatoes are finely diced, they will cook quickly. Add the spring onions and cook for a further 4-5 minutes. Add all the watercress with the stock and simmer over a low heat for 4-5 minutes. Season well. Blend the soup in a processor until smooth. Return to the saucepan, add a hint of lemon rind and a swirl of yoghurt then serve with chewy, crusty bread.

PARSNIP CHAMP WITH LEEKS, TURKEY RASHERS AND A HOME-MADE TOMATO SAUCE

Turkey rashers are a new food you will find in most supermarkets. Low in fat and easily cooked, these rashers are tasty and ideal to serve with champ as a quick snack.

Parsnip champ
450g/1lb parsnips
900g/2lb potatoes

2-3 leeks
30g/1oz mozzarella cheese

2 packets turkey rashers
2 dsp balsamic vinegar

Tomato sauce
1 clove garlic
1 onion, finely chopped
2 tsp tomato paste
450g/1lb tomatoes

1 tsp sugar
140ml/¼pt white wine or water
1 tsp fresh basil or thyme

Serves 6

Steam the parsnips and potatoes. The potatoes should take 20-25 minutes, the parsnips 15-20 minutes. Add the leeks in a separate steamer pan and cook for 5 minutes. Remove from heat. Mash the potatoes and parsnips together. Pile onto a plate and top with the leeks and grated

Overleaf: creamy watercress soup, parsnip champ

mozzarella. Brush the turkey rashers with balsamic vinegar and grill for 1-1½ minutes on both sides. The vinegar will improve the colour of the rashers. To make the tomato sauce, cook the garlic, onion and tomato paste on a dry pan for 2 minutes. Add the tomatoes, sugar, wine and thyme. Simmer for 25-30 minutes. This dish comes together in layers. Pile the parsnip mash onto a plate, top with the leeks, cheese and turkey rashers and spoon a little tomato sauce over the top.

A WINTER CITRUS FRUIT SALAD

When it comes to puddings, you are never stuck with whatever fruit is in season. The winter citrus fruits are so sharp and tangy in flavour, they make a refreshing end to any meal. Kumquat is now readily available and is a much undervalued fruit.

Sugar syrup:
550ml/1pt water
115g/4oz caster sugar

Fruits:
165g/6oz kumquats, sliced and stoned
assorted citrus fruits, approximately 6-8 fruits e.g. red grapefruit,
pink grapefruit, oranges, clementine, blood oranges

2 dsp Cointreau liqueur
1 lime, peel only
sprigs of mint

1 x 200g/7oz ice cream
55g/ 2oz muscavado sugar

Serves 8

Make the syrup by bubbling together the sugar and water. Add the sliced, stoned kumquats and bubble for 10 minutes, then cool. Prepare all the fruits, by peeling and removing the pith. Segment or slice all the fruit. Add the fruits to the cooled syrup. Add a dash of liqueur and decorate with lime peel and sprigs of mint. Serve with ice cream topped with muscavado sugar, flashed below a hot grill for 1-2 minutes.

A SPICY AROMATIC DRESSING

This sharp flavoured, tasty dressing is oil free and is ideal to serve at once, straight from the blender.

1 onion, finely chopped
1 dsp soft dark sugar
1 clove garlic, chopped
1" root ginger, chopped

2 dsp rice wine
salt and pepper
2 drops Tabasco

Serves 4

Place all the ingredients in a blender and whisk together to form a spicy, aromatic dressing.

A WARM, STICKY
ORANGE AND DATE PUDDING

This sponge pudding is made by a rather unusual method of creaming the sugar and egg together and folding in a small amount of fat with the flour. Use butter or polyunsaturated fat.

4 eggs
115g/4oz caster sugar
55g/ 4½oz self-raising flour, sieved
55g/2oz fat, softened
1 orange, rind only
30g/1oz dates, finely chopped
4 dsp orange marmalade
4 slices orange

TO SERVE 140ml/¼pt yoghurt

Serves 4

Beat together the eggs and sugar until white and creamy. Then add all the sieved flour, softened fat, orange rind and finely chopped dates. Carefully fold the mixture together and transfer to greased individual moulds. Line the moulds with 1 dsp of marmalade and a slice of orange. Fill ½-¾ of the mould with the sponge mixture. Place in a bain marie and cook in the oven at 375°F/190°C/gas number 5 for 15-20 minutes until cooked, puffed up and golden. Serve with a spoonful of yoghurt.

FAT FREE AND
FAST

———◆◆◆———

Good food that's fat free and cooked quickly is what a lot of us are looking for today.
When you are cooking in this way, the challenge is often to create meals that are healthy not filling, low in fat but tasty, full of flavour, and do not take all day to cook.

Fat in our diet tends to be addictive and many of the following recipes have reduced the fat and added the flavour with herbs, spices and oriental aromas.

A SPRING VEGETABLE SOUP

When it comes to making soup, a good home-made stock is essential. If you want a light flavoursome stock, then I think you will find chicken is hard to beat. After cooking, the stock should be chilled in the fridge overnight. Then you will find an amazing amount of fat can be removed by skimming the top.

Chicken Stock	
2.25L/4 pt water	2 stalks celery
4 chicken joints, 680g/1 ½lb	1 bunch parsley
1 onion	2 bay leaves
1 carrot	salt and pepper

1 dsp olive oil	½ leek
2 potatoes	2 spring onions
2 carrots	125g/4oz split peas, steeped in cold
2 stalks celery	water for 2 hours

Serves 8

Make the stock by adding to a large saucepan the water, chicken, onion, carrot, celery, parsley, bay leaves and seasoning. Simmer gently for 2 hours over a low heat then strain and chill in the fridge overnight. The fat can then be removed from the top. Start the soup by adding to the large saucepan 1 dsp of olive oil. Add the finely diced potato, carrot and celery and sweat together. Add the leek, spring onion, split peas and the strained stock, simmer gently for 10-15 minutes. Serve garnished with Parsley

STEAMED CELERIAC

Celeriac is a very unusual vegetable. It looks like a turnip and tastes faintly of celery. One of the best ways to cook it is simply to peel it, dice it and then steam it for 15 minutes and serve it with parsley and lemon.

1 celeriac, peeled and diced
2 dsp parsley, finely chopped
½ lemon, rind only

Serves 6

Place the peeled, diced celeriac in a steamer and cook for 15 minutes until tender. Sprinkle with finely chopped parsley and lemon rind. Serve hot.

MUSTARD SEED CHAMP

Champ in its many forms is creeping onto our menus. This is a wonderful, low fat version made with floury potatoes, whole grain mustard and fromage frais.

900g-1.3kg/2-3lb floury potatoes
1 tsp whole grain mustard
2 dsp fromage frais

Serves 8

Peel and cook the potatoes in boiling, salted water for 25 minutes. Drain and mash. Add the mustard and fromage frais then mix lightly together. Serve warm.

ORIENTAL FISH

The oriental way with fish is quick, tasty and simple with no deep fat frying. Instead the fish poaches in the sauce of garlic, ginger and soy sauce. The fish will hold its shape better if you leave the skin on.

2 fillets of sole or plaice, approximately 225g/8oz each

Sauce
1 tsp olive oil
2" root ginger
2 tsp soy sauce
1 lemon, juice and rind
2 cloves garlic
1 red chilli, chopped

1 green chilli, chopped
3-4 spring onions, chopped
1 red pepper, chopped
1 yellow pepper, chopped
1 orange pepper, chopped
1 stalk celery, sliced

Serves 2

Place the fish on an oiled grill pan and cook for 1-2 minutes. In a separate pan, with only a hint of oil, add the ginger, soy sauce, lemon rind and juice, garlic, chopped chillies, spring onions, peppers and celery. Toss around in the pan for 1-2 minutes. Add the fish to the pan skin-side down and continue to cook for a further 2 minutes. The thickness of the fish will affect the cooking time. Be careful, as cooking time of fish is short. Serve with cooked rice flavoured with lemon grass and parsley.

Overleaf: oriental fish

A FAMILY STYLE MINCE PIE WITH A ROAST POTATO TOPPING

If your family love red meat, there is no need to cut red meat out of your diet just because you are following the low fat way of eating. If it's mince steak you are using, you just need the right variety of mince. But one thing you will find, the better the quality, the lower the fat.

680g/1 ½lb lean mince steak	140 ml/ ¼ pint red wine
1 tsp olive oil	½ tsp oregano, dried
2 cloves garlic, chopped	140 ml/ ¼ pint vegetable stock
1 Spanish onion	4-6 potatoes, grated
2 tsp sun-dried tomato paste, remove excess oil	½ turnip, grated
2 tsp soy sauce	1 carrot, grated
2 tsp Worcestershire sauce	280 ml/ ½ pint fromage frais

Serves 8

Add the mince steak to a very hot non-stick pan and 1 tsp of olive oil. Cook for 2-3 minutes then add the garlic and onion and cook for 8-10 minutes over a high temperature. Add the tomato paste, soy sauce, Worcestershire sauce, red wine, oregano and stock. Reduce the heat and simmer for 30-40 minutes, then pour into a serving dish. Steam the vegetables for 3-4 minutes and allow to cool slightly before mixing with the fromage frais. Spoon over the cooked mince steak, sprinkle with paprika and black pepper. Cook in a pre-heated oven 375°F/190°C/gas number 5 for 30 minutes. Serve hot with a mixed leaf salad.

ROAST PIGEON BREASTS IN LEMON AND THYME

Pigeon breasts are low in fat, full of flavour and can be quickly cooked by roasting in the oven. There is no visible fat although they do need a little preparation in tidying up the breasts. Short cooking is all that is needed to cook these small breasts.

8-10 pigeon breasts

Marinade
140 ml/¼ pint red wine
1 lemon rind and juice
salt and pepper
1 dsp fresh thyme leaves

Serves 4

Place the cleaned and washed pigeon breasts in a bowl and pour over the marinade ingredients: wine, lemon juice, salt, pepper, lemon rind and thyme leaves. Cover with cling film and leave up to 24 hours in the fridge. Transfer the pigeon breasts and marinade to a foil-lined dish. Roast in the oven at 400°F/200°C/gas number 6 for 25-35 minutes. Serve hot with mustard seed champ and steamed celeriac.

A CRUNCHY PEAR MERINGUE

This is a very simple pudding made by combining lightly poached pears with a crunchy meringue.

6-8 pears, peeled and cut into halves

Syrup
280 ml/1/2 pint water
280 ml/1/2 pint red wine
55g-225g/2-4oz caster sugar

1 cinnamon stick
2 dsp lemon juice

Crunchy Meringue
3 egg whites
165g/6oz caster sugar
30g/1oz amaretto biscuits, lightly crushed

Serves 6

Place the peeled pear halves into the syrup. The syrup is made by bubbling together the water, wine, sugar, cinnamon stick and lemon juice together until the sugar has dissolved. Cook the pears over a low heat for 5-6 minutes approximately but be careful not to overcook as they will become soft very easily. Beat the egg whites with half the sugar until stiff and forming peaks. Fold in the remainder of the sugar and the lightly crushed amaretto biscuits. Spoon on top of the pears and cook in a hot oven at 425°F/220°C/gas number 7 for 5-6 minutes. Serve with yoghurt or low fat fromage frais.

A WARM BAKED PEAR PUDDING

When it comes to puddings, there is no need to cut them out just because you are trying to watch the fat in your diet. Fresh fruit is ideal and can be cooked in so many ways. For a simple pudding try this crumbly topping made with reduced fat biscuits on pears.

6-8 pears
2-3 dsp orange juice

2 dsp apricot jam
30g/1oz demerara sugar

Crumble Topping
170g/6oz low/reduced fat digestive biscuits
1/2 tsp cinnamon powder
1 orange, peel only

55g/2oz sultanas
2 dsp honey, heated

TO SERVE: *115g/4oz yoghurt*

Serves 6

Peel, core and slice the pears and arrange in an oven proof dish. Sprinkle with orange juice to bake, then softened apricot jam to glaze and a hint of demerara sugar to sweeten if you wish. Crush the biscuits finely and place in a large mixing bowl. Add the cinnamon powder, orange peel, sultanas and heated honey. Mix well together to form a crumble then spoon on top of the pudding. Smooth the top and bake in the oven at 400°F/200°C/gas number 6 for 20 minutes until the pears are cooked and the topping crumbly. Serve with yoghurt.

SIMPLY SNACKING

S nacking is now a way of life but today it is becoming a more healthy way to eat. It does not involve quick, unhealthy cooking methods but combines healthy breads, fresh fruit, fish toppings and lower fat alternatives served as snacks.

CHICKEN WITH A TANGY LEMON AND GINGER SAUCE

Here is a very spicy, tangy sauce almost Oriental in appearance, yet sweet and delicious. Try serving this dish with couscous flavoured with spring onion for a light accompaniment. The balsamic vinegar works well as an instant marinade.

1 chicken fillet
1 dsp balsamic vinegar
1 dsp oil
15g/¹/₂oz butter
1 clove garlic
1" root ginger
2 spring onions

1 dsp honey
1 lemon, rind & juice only
140ml/¹/₄pt stock
1 dsp lemon marmalade
salt and pepper
1 dsp soy sauce

TO SERVE: parsley, finely chopped

Serves 1

Toss the chicken fillet in balsamic vinegar, then cook in the pan in oil and butter for 1-2 minutes until well cooked. Add the garlic, ginger, spring onion and cook for 1 minute. Then add the honey, lemon and stock and simmer for 6 minutes until the sauce has reduced and the chicken is almost cooked. Add the lemon marmalade to thicken the sauce, salt, pepper and soy sauce and heat thoroughly. Serve garnished with parsley.

CHICKEN WITH AN ORANGE AND MUSTARD SAUCE

Chicken fillets are so quick and easy to cook. If you cook them in a pan with a little oil and butter, then the juices can be used to make a quick, tasty sauce.

1 chicken fillet
15g/¹/₂oz butter
1 dsp oil
70 ml/¹/₈pt orange juice

1 orange, rind and segments
1 tsp mustard/1 whole grain
70 ml/¹/₈pt chicken stock

Serves 1

Flatten the chicken fillet, then fry in the pan with the butter and oil until golden on both sides. Add the orange juice, rind, segments, mustard and stock and heat thoroughly for 2-3 minutes until the sauce has thickened and reduced. The whole grain mustard will thicken the sauce and give a creamy texture. This dish is very good served with baby potatoes tossed in buttered chives.

CHICKEN WITH A SUN-DRIED TOMATO SAUCE

Chicken is invaluable when cooking something for the family that is quick and tasty. This dish does not involve marinading but is packed full of flavour with the sun-dried tomatoes, dried herbs and spring onions.

3 chicken fillets
1 red onion

1 tsp olive oil
4 spring onions

1 red pepper
1 yellow pepper
1 dsp sun-dried tomatoes
1/2 tsp oregano
140 ml/¼pt chicken stock

140 ml/¼pt dry white wine
115g/4oz green grapes
115g/4oz black grapes
1 dsp parsley, finely chopped

Serves 3

Cut the chicken fillets into strips. Slice the onion into rings and cook in the pan with the oil and then add the spring onion. Add the chicken strips and brown for 2-3 minutes. Add the peppers and continue to cook for 2 minutes until lightly softened. Next in with the flavours. Add the sun-dried tomatoes, the oregano, stock and wine and leave to simmer for 8-10 minutes. Finally, add the grapes and parsley. Heat thoroughly for 2-3 minutes. Over-cooking the grapes will spoil the final appearance of this dish. Then serve.

FLOURY BAPS WITH
BRIE AND TOASTED PEARS

Bread and cheese make a very tasty snack. When you vary the bread to floury baps and the cheese to creamy brie or Wensleydale, you have a tasty snack topped with cranberries or blueberries. I like the flavour of brie and pears together.

4 floury baps
115g/4oz cranberries
2 dsp water
30g/1oz demerara sugar

½ orange, peel only
2 pears, peeled & sliced
1 dsp honey
115g/4oz brie cheese, cut into slices

Serves 4

Slice baps by cutting off tops, butter and toast below a hot grill. Leave to cool. Peel and slice the pears. Layer on top of the toasted baps and sprinkle with honey. Arrange slices of cheese on top and grill until bubbling and golden. To make the sauce, poach the berries in water, sugar and orange peel for 6-7 minutes until soft and beginning to pop. Serve baps warm with a spoonful of cranberry sauce.

A QUICK BREAD-BASED PIZZA

If it's a quick pizza you're after, use a bought bread base and cook this pizza below the grill for a tasty snack in minutes. Choose a bread flavoured with olives, tomatoes, herbs or spices.

1 pizza base or bought bread
2 dsp olive oil
1 dsp sun-dried tomato paste
115g/4oz tomatoes

4-5 slices Parma ham
115g/4oz mozzarella cheese
black pepper
1 red onion

Serves 4

Warm the bread base in a hot oven for 5-6 minutes. Sprinkle with olive oil and spread the tomato paste over the top. Arrange the sliced tomatoes, Parma ham and cheese over the top. Sprinkle with black pepper and place under a hot grill for 2-3 minutes until the cheese has become melted and golden. Cut the onion into rings, then fry until crispy and place on top of pizza. Serve warm.

Overleaf: chicken with a tangy lemon & ginger sauce, chicken with a sun-dried tomato sauce

PEPPER-CRUSTED MONKFISH IN A PROVENÇALE SAUCE

Fish is ideal if it is a quick meal you're after and a fish such as monkfish cooks easily. In this recipe, the large cubes are tossed in dried spices, then cooked in garlic and tomatoes to give a very tasty sauce. The secret of monkfish lies in the freshness. Ask your fishmonger to prepare it well for you, removing the skin, membrane and central bone.

680g/1½lb monkfish, cubed
1 dsp peppercorns, crushed
1 tsp chilli flakes
1 tsp paprika pepper
1 dsp olive oil

1 clove garlic
400g/14oz can tomatoes
140 ml/¼pt white wine
olives

TO SERVE: 2 dsp parsley, finely chopped

Serves 4-6

Prepare the monkfish tails and cut up into cubes. Toss in the pepper, chilli flakes, paprika and pat down well. Heat the oil in the pan and cook the garlic for 1-2 minutes. Add the cubes of fish and toss around. When it becomes opaque, approximately 3-4 minutes, add the tomatoes, wine and olives. This only takes several minutes to cook as a dish like this spoils if the fish is over-cooked. Serve hot. Garnish with parsley.

CHICKEN IN A WARM PEPPERCORN SAUCE

Peppercorns have a hot, spicy flavour. Black peppercorns are the hottest of all but the pink look super for colour in this creamy sauce.

1 chicken fillet
30g/1oz butter
1 dsp olive oil
1 tsp each peppercorns, pink, black, green

70 ml/⅛pt crème fraîche
70 ml/⅛pt yoghurt
1 tsp parsley, finely chopped

Serves 1

Cook the chicken fillet in the oil and butter but do not let it brown. Cook for 6-7 minutes until the fillet is tender and almost cooked. Add the crushed peppercorns and the mixed crème fraîche and yoghurt. Heat thoroughly, but gently and do not allow the sauce to boil. Serve garnished with parsley and crusty bread.

FRESH RASPBERRIES WITH A WHITE CHOCOLATE & MARSHMALLOW SAUCE

Chocolate sauce poured over fresh berries is just delicious, so to ring the changes, here is a very simple recipe for a white chocolate sauce mixed with softened marshmallows and served warm. Be careful not to over-heat the chocolate or it will curdle and separate. Serve at once or the sauce will firm as it cools.

Chocolate sauce
115g/4oz white chocolate, melted
55g/2oz marshmallows
15g/½oz butter

2 dsp cream
225g/8oz fresh raspberries
1 tsp sugar

Serves 2-3

Melt the chocolate in a bowl over hot water. Add the marshmallows, butter and cream. The heat will be sufficient to melt the butter and soften the marshmallows. Do not over-heat. Spoon the raspberries into tall glasses, spoon over a little sugar and serve with the hot marshmallow sauce over the top. Serve at once.

A FRESH RASPBERRY AND FILO TART

Fresh fruit is an easy answer to quick puddings and here is a simple tart made with fresh raspberries, tinned peaches and a casing of filo pastry. This pie cooks in the oven in 15 minutes. If you prefer, use puff pastry, but it takes a little longer to cook. Raspberries are such a tasty fruit and combine well with kiwi, cherries and nectarines.

4 sheets filo pastry　　　　　　　　*225g/8oz raspberries*
15g/¹⁄2oz butter　　　　　　　　　*2 dsp peach jam*
1 dsp oil　　　　　　　　　　　　*30g/1oz icing sugar*
400g/14oz can fruit　　　　　　　*yoghurt or whipped cream*

Serves 6

Brush the sheets of pastry with the butter and oil and layer the flan tins with 4 sheets. Sprinkle with the drained fruit and raspberries and spread over the peach jam. Cook in the oven at 400°F/200° C/gas number 6 for 15 minutes. Sprinkle with icing sugar. Serve with yoghurt or whipped cream.

RASPBERRIES WITH HOT SUGARED MASCARPONE

A very easy, quick pudding made with fresh or frozen berries and topped with mascarpone and yoghurt. The yoghurt lowers the fat content of this pudding when mixed with the mascarpone cheese. The flavour and the texture of mascarpone cheese is delicious in puddings.

450g/1lb raspberries, fresh　　　　*115g/4 oz yoghurt*
15g/1/2oz demerara sugar　　　　　*115g-170g/4-6oz mascarpone cheese*

Topping
30g/1oz demerara or icing sugar　　*30g/1oz raspberries*
30g/1oz hazelnuts, chopped　　　　*sprigs of mint*

Serves 6-8

Spoon the washed berries into a bowl and top with the sugar. Mix together the yoghurt and the mascarpone cheese, then spoon on top of the raspberries. Dust with sugar and flash below a very hot grill for approximately 2 minutes until bubbling and golden. Serve hot with chopped hazelnuts, raspberries and sprigs of mint.

Overleaf: raspberries with hot sugared mascarpone, fresh raspberries with a white chocolate and marshmallow sauce

...ND MUSHROOM PIE

...astry topping is the sort of fare the family love.
... the fat in the fridge before grating it into the
...are well worth the making for a comforting,

cold water to mix to a soft dough
900g/2lb steak pieces

1 dsp Worcestershire sauce
salt and pepper

250ml/1½pt stock
30g/1oz flour & 2 dsp warm water, blended
1 egg, lightly beaten

...ves 8

...t into the flour, chop thoroughly with a knife
...for ½ hour. Cut the steak into pieces and place
...orcestershire sauce and seasoning, toss around
...nutes–1 hour). This will improve the texture,
...the meat in batches in the pan with just a hint
...vour. When all has been browned, pour in the
...ed onion and mushrooms, the stock, seasoning
...thickens, then transfer to an ovenproof dish.
...k. Brush with lightly beaten egg and use the
...with beaten egg. Cook in the oven at
...d reduce to 400°F/200°C/gas number 6 for 20

...ASTA SOUP

...ds to sustain energy. Here is a pasta and fresh
...icious served with warm, crusty bread, topped

1 bay leaf
140 ml/¼pt white wine
1.1L/2pt stock, beef or vegetable
115g/4oz pasta shapes
salt
2 dsp parsley

A TASTY STEAK AI

A tasty steak and mushroom pie with a golden
This is a quick pastry and it is important to chi
flour. Most pastries have a high fat content, but
filling, family style meal.

450g/1lb plain flour
¹/₂ tsp salt
340g/12oz fat, chilled & grated

Marinade
2 dsp balsamic vinegar
1 dsp oil

---

1 dsp olive oil
1 onion
225g/¹/₂lb mushrooms

Ser

Sieve the flour and salt into a bowl. Grate the f
and mix with water to form a soft dough. Relax
in a bowl, to marinade. Add the vinegar, oil, W
and leave to marinade as long as possible (15 m
flavour and cooking qualities of the meat. Cook
of olive oil to brown the meat and seal in the fl
remainder of the marinade. Add the lightly coo
and blended flour. Cook for 1-2 minutes until it
Cover with the pastry, rolled out to ¹/₂ inch thic
remainder of pastry to make pastry leaves. Brus
450°F/230°C/gas number 9 for 10-15 minutes a
minutes. Serve hot.

A QUICK P.

A good robust bowl of soup is one of the best fo
vegetable soup that cooks in 15 minutes. It is de
with Parmesan cheese.

1 tsp olive oil
2 cloves garlic
1 leek, finely sliced
2 stalks celery
2 courgettes
44g/1x14oz can tomatoes
400g can cannelloni beans

TO SERVE: crusty bread, 55g/2oz Parmesan cheese

Serves 6-8

Cook the oil and garlic together for 1-2 minutes. Then add the sliced leek, celery and courgettes and cook for 2-3 minutes without the lid on top. Add the tomatoes and beans, bay leaf, wine and stock and stir well. Add the pasta shapes and seasoning and cook for 10-12 minutes. Several minutes before the soup is cooked, add the finely chopped parsley. Serve with crusty bread topped with Parmesan.

A VERY FRUITY BREAD PUDDING

A low fat, high energy pudding packed with a variety of dried fruits, such as mangos, peaches, pears, pineapples, dates and sultanas. This pudding is made with spongy brioche and does not need to be buttered. For a healthier version, make the pudding with low fat milk.

1 loaf, sliced	55g/2oz sultanas
55g/2oz dried pears	55g/2oz dates, chopped
55g/2oz dried mangos	2-3 dsp sherry
55g/2oz dried pineapple	1/2 tsp cinnamon

Custard
570ml/1 pt milk, low fat	30g/1oz caster sugar
4-5 egg yolks, lightly beaten	1/2 tsp cinnamon powder

Serves 8

Arrange slices of bread in an ovenproof dish. Place the dried fruits in a bowl with the sherry and cinnamon. Stir around and leave to sit for 5-10 minutes. The fruits will absorb the liquid and soften. Pour over the bread. Make the custard by mixing together the milk, lightly beaten egg yolks, sugar and cinnamon in a saucepan over a low heat. Do not allow the mixture to boil or it will curdle, but when it shows signs of thickening, remove from the heat and pour over the bread. Leave to sit for 10 minutes before baking in the oven at 375°F/190°C/gas number 5 for 25-30 minutes. Serve warm.

A CHERRY CHERRY CAKE

Grains of all kinds are great sources of energy and here is the latest one to come our way. Polenta with its bright yellow colour can be used to make a pie with an unusual crumbly texture. The filling for this pie can be made with cherries, raspberries, apples or plums.

225g/8oz plain flour	55g/2 oz sugar
115g/4oz polenta	1 egg, lightly beaten
1 tsp baking powder	115g/4oz butter, softened
1 lemon, rind & juice	

Filling
2 x 450g/1lb can cherries, stoned	1 dsp water
30g/1oz arrowroot	

Overleaf: a cherry cherry cake

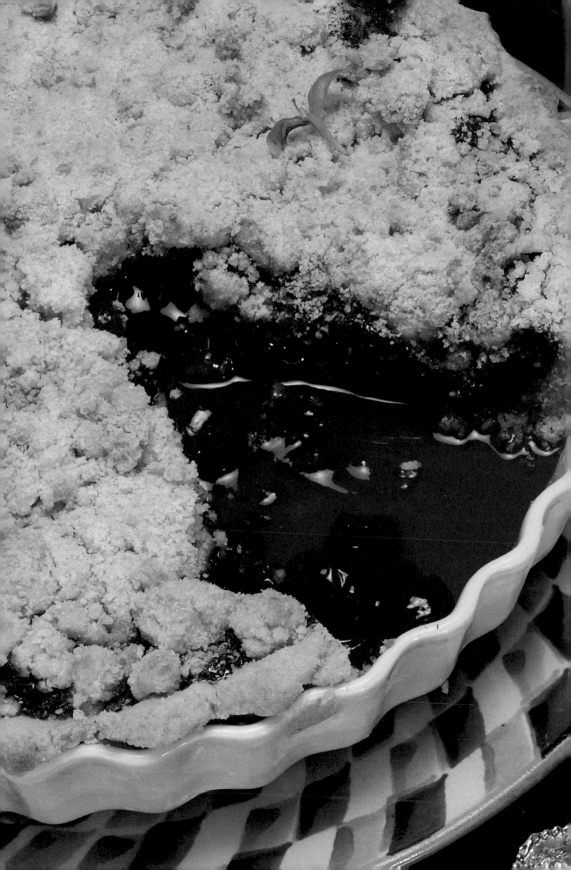

Serves 8-10

Into the blender add the first seven ingredients and blend together until the mixture becomes crumbly yet firm. Use ²/₃ of this mixture to line a 7-8 inch loose bottomed flan dish. Take time to press this down well and onto the sides and keep the remaining ¹/₃ to crumble over the top. Add the cherries to a saucepan and then add the blended arrowroot. Bring to the boil and stir until the mixture thickens. Allow to cool slightly, then pour over the base. Sprinkle the remainder of the crumble over the top. Spread out evenly and bake in the oven at 350°F/180°C/gas number 4 for 30-35 minutes. Leave to cool before un-moulding, then serve with yoghurt.

BUTTERMILK WHEATEN LOAVES

When you are looking for something to boost the energy and fill a space, then a bread that is simple to make can be just ideal. Here is a basic loaf that can be either sweet or savoury depending upon which ingredients you choose to add.

225g/8oz plain flour	
225g/8oz wheaten meal flour	*15g/¹/₂oz butter*
1 level tsp baking soda	*1 dsp honey*
¹/₄ tsp salt	

Savoury	
85g/3oz mozzarella cheese, sliced	*1 dsp parsley*
2 rashers bacon, cooked & sliced	

Sweet	
55g/2oz sultanas	*30g/1oz hazelnuts*
55g/2oz dates	

425ml/³/₄pt buttermilk

Serves 8

Sieve the plain flour into a bowl. Add the wheaten meal flour and mix. Add the baking soda, salt and then cut and rub in the butter until it crumbles into the mixture. Add the honey. This is a flavoured wheaten loaf so next in with the flavourings. For the savoury loaf add the cheese, bacon and parsley. For the sweet loaf, add the sultanas, date and hazelnuts. Add the buttermilk quickly and mix until it forms a soft sticky dough. Transfer to a lightly greased loaf tin and flatten the top. Sprinkle with a little of the remaining cheese or hazelnuts, depending on which loaf is being made. Then bake in the oven at 425°F/220°C/gas number 7 for 25-30 minutes.

CHICKEN WITH SUN-DRIED TOMATOES AND MOZZARELLA SAUCE

A chicken and potato topped pie is always a firm favourite. This one is topped with light soufflé potatoes and flavoured with sun-dried tomatoes and mozzarella cheese sauce. Sun-dried tomatoes, mozzarella cheese and oregano are flavours that we have become accustomed to as pizza toppings.

4 chicken fillets
1 dsp olive oil
4-6 spring onions, sliced

2-3 dsp sun-dried tomatoes
½ tsp oregano, dried

Sauce
280 ml/½pt low fat milk
1 dsp olive oil
3oz mozzarella cheese

1oz plain flour
3-4 rashers bacon, cooked & sliced

Topping
900g/2lb potatoes, peeled
2 egg whites, beaten
2 dsp low fat milk

TO SERVE: parsley, finely chopped

Serves 4-6

Cook the chicken in a pan with a little oil. Add the spring onion and cook for several minutes. Add the sliced sun-dried tomatoes and a little oregano; when almost cooked, pour onto a serving· dish. To make the sauce, heat all the sauce ingredients together, milk, oil, cheese and flour, for 1 minute until it bubbles and thickens. Add the cooked bacon and pour over the chicken. Boil the potatoes for 20-25 minutes until soft, drain and mash with the low fat milk. Add the beaten egg whites and fold in carefully to lighten the potatoes. Spoon over the pie and bake in the oven at 400°F/200°C/gas number 6 for 20-25 minutes to crisp up the potatoes and heat the pie thoroughly. Garnish with parsley and serve with baby tomatoes roasted in the oven for 15 minutes sprinkled with 2 dsp olive oil, 1 dsp honey and 1 dsp balsamic vinegar at 400°F/200°C/gas number 6 for 15 minutes, or just until they soften, pop and blacken.

GOOD
FAST FOOD

———◆———

D oes your family consider fast food to be
a portion of fish and chips, a burger, a
frozen tv dinner or a takeaway Chinese
meal? With a little planning and some
careful shopping, fast food can mean meals packed
with vitamins and goodness.

Cooking methods have become much quicker and
healthier which suits today's hectic lifestyle.

You will be surprised that these recipes can be
made in the same space of time it takes to reheat
a frozen dinner or queue for fish and chips.

CRUSTED POTATO WEDGES

Potato wedges, in our house, are becoming as popular as chipped potatoes as they are quick to prepare and healthier to cook. The sauce is made by the "all-in-one" method with low fat milk, olive oil and either mature or low fat cheese.

4-5 potatoes, cut into wedges

Sauce
570 ml/1pt milk, low fat
30g/1oz plain flour
55g/2oz cheddar cheese, mature

salt and pepper
1 dsp olive oil

1 dsp spring onions, finely chopped

Serves 4

Steam the potatoes for 6-7 minutes, then transfer to a lightly oiled ovenproof dish. To make the sauce, place all the sauce ingredients in a saucepan and, whisking all the time, bring to the boil and cook for 1 minute. Add the finely chopped spring onions and pour over the potatoes. Bake in the oven at 400°F/200°C/gas number 6 for 20 minutes approximately until bubbling and cooked. Serve hot.

A CRUSTED SPICED COD

Fish and chips are just so popular but, by changing the way you cook them, you can have a much faster and healthier result. Instead of coating with batter, a crumbed, crusted topping is placed on top and the fish then roasted in the oven.

115g/4 x 4oz cod fillets

2 dsp lemon juice

Crusted Topping
115g/4oz white breadcrumbs
1 dsp olive oil
2 dsp spring onions, finely chopped

1 tsp paprika pepper
salt and pepper
1 tsp peppercorns, crushed

1 dsp olive oil
15g/1/2oz butter or polyunsaturated fat

Serves 4

Sprinkle the fish with lemon juice and leave to sit for a few minutes to improve the flavour. Toss the breadcrumbs in olive oil, add the finely chopped spring onions, paprika, seasoning and peppercorns. Mix well together, then divide over the cod fillets. Cook in a hot pan with 1 dsp olive oil and butter for 2 minutes, just until the base of the fish is sealed. Transfer to a hot oven and bake at 400°F/200°C/gas number 6 for 8-10 minutes or until the fish is cooked through. The cooking time will vary with the thickness of the fish. Serve at once.

A ROASTED MEDITERRANEAN SALSA

Roasted vegetables are so quick and easy to cook in the oven, and there is such a wide selection to choose from today. During cooking this dish takes on a wonderful flavour and the texture of the crispy blackened vegetables is so good. Vary the vegetables with whatever is in season.

1 aubergine	2 dsp lemon juice
1 courgette	2 dsp balsamic vinegar
1 yellow pepper	2 dsp olive oil
1 red onion	salt and pepper
4-5 spring onions	1/2 tsp oregano, dried
225g/8oz baby tomatoes	

TO SERVE: parsley

Serves 4-6

Cut the vegetables into pieces and arrange in an ovenproof dish. Keep the vegetables in chunky pieces for a more attractive salsa. Sprinkle with lemon juice, balsamic vinegar, olive oil, salt and pepper and, finally, a sprinkle of dried or fresh oregano. Toss all the vegetables in the oil and vinegar before cooking in the oven at 400°F/200°C/gas number 6 for 20-25 minutes until softened, blackened and cooked. Serve warm sprinkled with parsley.

EASTERN FLAVOURED COUSCOUS

Couscous is one of the most popular "new" foods we have. A grain that resembles pasta and is similar to semolina, it absorbs the flavour of whatever stock you add and can be served either warm or cold. Just watch how it swells up and absorbs the liquid.

570ml/1pt chicken stock	55g/2oz dried apricots, shredded
225g/8oz couscous	30g/1oz almonds
115g/4oz can chick peas	2 dsp mint, coarsely chopped

Serves 4-6

Pour the stock over the couscous and leave to sit for 8-10 minutes until it absorbs the liquid and doubles in size. Add the drained chick peas, dried apricots, almonds and mint.
Toss around and serve warm or chilled.

A BACON, BRIE AND FILO TART

This is a delicately flavoured, savoury tart that is ideal as a starter, light lunch or an evening meal. The filling is light and creamy with the crispy, cooked bacon and flavoursome sun-dried tomatoes. Try brushing the pastry with egg white and oil instead of butter for a less calorific result.

4 sheets filo pastry	225g/8oz brie cheese, cut into chunks
1 egg white	115g/4oz bacon, lightly grilled
1 dsp olive oil	55g/2oz sun-dried tomatoes, shredded

Topping

115g/4oz low fat yoghurt	salt and pepper
4 dsp milk or cream	1/2 tsp paprika pepper
2 egg yolks	

Serves 6-8

Layer the sheets of filo pastry and brush in between each with egg white and olive oil. Layer well into the tin and press well into the corners. Make in a round, square or rectangular tin. Cut the

Overleaf: bacon, brie and filo tart

cheese into chunks and scatter over the pastry-lined tin. Scatter the bacon and shredded tomatoes over the top. Make the topping by mixing together the yoghurt, milk, egg yolks, salt, pepper and paprika. Pour over the tart and bake in the oven at 375°F/190°C/gas number 5 for 20-25 minutes. Serve hot or cold, with salad or baked potatoes.

STEAK AND ONION SANDWICH

When it comes to a quick snack, then you can't beat a sandwich. How the sandwich has changed! Today there are breads, fillings and flavours from every corner of the world, giving flavours and textures to tempt the hungry.

1 small loaf, e.g. Ciabatta	1 dsp balsamic vinegar
mustard	few drops Worcestershire sauce
450g/1lb fillet steak	pickles, relish
1 dsp olive oil	1 red onion
15g/¹/2oz butter	

TO SERVE: parsley; 1 tomato, sliced

Serves 4

Cut the bread in half, lengthways, and toast. Spread with mustard. Cut the steak into fine slices and flash in a hot pan of oil and butter. Cook for 1 minute on each side. Add the balsamic vinegar and Worcestershire sauce. Fry the onion rings for 2-3 minutes. Assemble the sandwich together. Top with pickles, steak and onion, then garnish with parsley and tomato slices.

A PERSIAN FLAVOURED CHICKEN DISH

When it comes to cooking good food fast, then I find chicken fillets are invaluable as they have no preparation, little wastage and, best of all, they are low in fat. This dish has a hint of Persian cooking which means it is sweet, aromatic and spicy.

4 chicken fillets	1 onion, finely chopped
1 tsp cinnamon powder	30g/1oz soft brown sugar
1 tsp turmeric powder	140 ml/¹/4pt orange juice
1 tsp paprika pepper	2 dsp lemon juice
salt and pepper	140 ml/¹/4pt chicken stock
30g/1oz butter	1 orange, rind only
1 dsp olive oil	30g/1oz almond flakes

TO SERVE: 1 dsp parsley, chopped

Serves 4

Trim any excess fat from the fillets and toss in the spices. If preferred, the chicken can be cut into large, chunky pieces. Melt the butter in the frying pan, add the oil and onion and cook until softened, 2-3 minutes. Add the soft brown sugar and chicken fillets and cook well on both sides for 2-3 minutes to seal the spices. Add the orange juice, lemon juice and stock and cook for 10-12 minutes. During this time the sauce will become thick and syrupy.
Add a little orange rind and a few flaked almonds and garnish with finely chopped parsley.

WARM BERRIES IN AN IRISH LIQUEUR

A warm yoghurt pudding with berries tossed in an Irish liqueur and sweetened with icing sugar.

Choose berries that are firm in texture and not over-ripe.

450g/1lb berries,
strawberries, raspberries and blueberries
30g/1oz icing sugar
hint of Irish Mist

1 egg yolk
225g/8oz yoghurt
1 dsp honey
30g/1oz demerara sugar

Serves 4

Mix together the berries in a bowl with the icing sugar and liqueur. Transfer to an ovenproof dish. Mix together the egg yolk, yoghurt and honey until smooth, then pour over the fruits on the plate. Scatter with demerara sugar and cook below a hot grill for 2-3 minutes until bubbling and golden.

A RASPBERRY, ALMOND AND YOGHURT PUDDING

Raspberries, almond biscuits and yoghurt combine well together to make a very fast pudding with a crunchy texture. However, if this pudding is to be made well in advance, then fresh raspberries will give a better result. Add a little sugar to sweeten if the raspberries are not completely ripe.

225g/8oz raspberries
115g/4oz almond biscuits
115g/4oz Greek yoghurt

30g/1oz almonds, flaked
sprig of mint

Serves 2

Combine together the fresh or frozen raspberries, crushed almond biscuits and yoghurt. Spoon into individual glasses on top of a few raspberries and swirl around to give a marbling effect. Decorate with a few fresh berries, flaked almonds and a sprig of mint. Serve chilled.

A YOGHURT LAYERED CAKE

Yoghurt, crème fraîche and fromage frais make the most delicious and simple of puddings if combined with fresh fruit. This one can either be made with fine slices of Madeira cake or sponge fingers sandwiched together.

55g/2oz cream cheese
225g/8oz yoghurt
2 passion fruits, juice and seeds
1 peach, diced and peeled
2-3 dsp Cointreau liqueur

1 packet sponge fingers
1 peach, sliced
1 mango, cut into slices
2-3 plums, cut into slices
1 star fruit, cut into slices

Serves 6

Make the filling by creaming together the cream cheese, yoghurt, passion fruit juice and seeds, and diced peach. Layer the sponge fingers on to a plate and top with half of filling. Repeat this process, another layer of sponge finger, another layer of yoghurt mixture. If you like, a little concentrated orange liqueur can be sprinkled over the sponge fingers to add extra flavour. Decorate the pudding with slices of peach, mango, plums and star fruit.

Overleaf: raspberry, almond and yoghurt pudding, yoghurt layered cake

SPEEDY SNACKING

S nacking is now a healthy way of life. It does not mean resorting to a bar of chocolate or a bag of crisps to satisfy hunger. Pancakes, pasta and breads with cheese and vegetable toppings are healthy, tasty snacks which can be made in minutes.

PAN-FRIED PARSNIPS

A quick, tasty way to cook parsnips.

4 parsnips, grated
1 apple, grated

1 dsp olive oil
140ml/¼ pt single cream

TO SERVE 1 dsp parsley

Serves 4

Grate the parsnip and apple and cook the parsnip in a shallow pan in 1 dsp olive oil for 1-2 minutes until softened. Add the grated apple and cream and heat for 1-2 minutes until the cream has been absorbed. Garnish with parsley.

CRAB AND POTATO CAKES

There always seem to be a couple of potatoes left over in the pan and, if you combine them with a can of fish, you can make the tastiest of fish dishes.

225g/8oz potatoes cooked & mashed
225g/8oz crab meat, tinned & drained
1 dsp parsley
1 dsp spring onion, finely chopped

1 egg, lightly beaten
30g/1oz grated cheddar cheese
salt and pepper

To coat
30g/1oz flour
115g/4oz matzo meal or wholemeal flour

Serves 4

Mash the cooked potatoes and mix with the cooked, drained crab meat. Add the parsley, spring onion, egg, cheese and seasoning. Mix well until it all binds together. Dust your hands lightly with flour and shape the mixture into four rounds. Coat with matzo meal and shake off any excess, then cook under the grill, bake in the oven or fry in the pan for 3 minutes on either side. Serve hot with salad or a spoonful of corn relish.

POTATO PANCAKES WITH
SOURED CREAM & SMOKED SALMON

Grated potato cooks so much quicker than whole potatoes, boiled or roasted. Use grated potato to make pancakes which cook quickly.

3-4 potatoes
½ onion, finely chopped
2 dsp flour, plain or wholemeal

1 egg
salt

TO SERVE: 1 tub soured cream, 4 slices smoked salmon, chopped dill

Serves 4

Grate the potatoes into a sieve and squeeze out as much moisture as possible. Add the chopped onion and continue to squeeze any moisture from the onion. Add the flour, seasoning and egg and mix well. Add 1dsp of the mixture to the pan in individual cakes and cook the pancakes on the pan with a hint of oil. Cook for 1½ minutes on both sides, then drain on kitchen paper. Serve topped with soured cream, dill and smoked salmon.

SPANISH SAUSAGE WITH LINGUINE

Sausages are a great snack food but, if you fancy one that is tasty and spicy, then try the Chorizo, a Spanish variety flavoured with cayenne. It is most often dried and smoked.

450g/1lb pasta, fresh or dried
1 dsp oil
1 onion, cut into rings
2 rashers bacon

1 dsp olive oil
2 Chorizo sausages, sliced
1 x 225g/8oz packet pancetta
2 fresh tomatoes, chopped

Serves 4

Cook the pasta in boiling, salted water and 1 dsp oil for 6-7 minutes. Then drain. In a separate pan, cook the onion and bacon in olive oil until crispy. Add the sliced sausage, pancetta and fresh tomatoes. Heat thoroughly for 2-3 minutes. Then serve with the drained pasta. Garnish with parsley.

IRISH SODA BREAD TOPPED WITH SALAMI AND OLIVES

Soda bread can be served in many ways as a snack. Try this tasty version, topped with salami.

Soda bread
55g/2oz cheddar cheese
1 dsp mayonnaise

1 dsp chives
6-8 slices salami
4-6 olives

Serves 2

Cut the soda bread in half and top with cheese, mayonnaise and chives mixed together. Grill for 2 minutes until bubbly and golden. The mayonnaise will help the cheese to bubble. Top with sliced salami and sliced olives.

Overleaf: Spanish sausage with linguine, Irish soda bread topped with salami and olives

TOASTED BRUSCHETTA WITH CHARGRILLED VEGETABLES

Crusty bread is ideal for bruschetta and can simply be topped with chargrilled vegetables.

1 crusty loaf
olive oil

garlic, finely chopped

Topping
assorted vegetables, e.g.peppers,
onions, courgettes, spring onions
1 dsp basil, finely chopped

2 dsp mayonnaise
2 dsp low fat yoghurt
olive oil

Serves 2

Cut the crusty bread into slices. Sprinkle with olive oil and garlic and grill. Cut the vegetables into good sized chunky pieces and place on an oiled grill pan. Cook for 2 minutes until slightly softened. Place the cooked vegetables on top of the bruschetta and top with basil mixed with mayonnaise, yoghurt and finely chopped herbs.

FLOURY BAPS WITH TOMATO AND MELTING CHEESE

Floury baps toast beautifully, retain their springiness and are great to serve with tomato and cheese.

3 baps
3 tsp sun-dried tomato paste

6 slices tomato
100g/4oz mozzarella cheese

TO SERVE: 3 dsp onion relish, 3 slices tomato

Serves 3

Cut the tops off the baps and toast them under the grill. Spread with sun-dried tomato paste and top with tomato slices and mozzarella cheese alternately. Place below a hot grill until the cheese is melted and golden. Serve warm, topped with onion relish and tomato.

TOASTED VEDA BREAD TOPPED WITH BLACKENED AUTUMN PLUMS

Veda loaf with its malt flavour, crusty top and chewy texture is an old time favourite. If you fancy something sweet for a snack, then Veda bread topped with autumn fruit is delicious.

2 thick slices Veda bread
6-8 plums, damsons or greengargus
2 dsp water
1 dsp honey

30g/1oz demerara sugar
pinch cinnamon or nutmeg
a few flaked almonds

TO SERVE: 1 dsp yoghurt

Serves 2

Toast the bread on both sides. Poach the fruit in the water, honey, sugar and cinnamon for 3-4 minutes until slightly softened, then leave to cool. Spoon over the bread, top with almonds and a hint of sugar. Flash below a hot grill and serve hot with yoghurt.

A SAUSAGE AND APPLE CASSEROLE

Sausages cook beautifully if you caramelise them in the pan with butter and a hint of brown sugar. This dish combines easily with apples and mushrooms to form a wonderfully simple casserole, ideal for any family.

450g/1lb pork sausages
30g/1oz butter
30g/1oz demerara sugar
1 red onion, cut into rings
1 white onion, cut into rings
115g/4oz button mushrooms, whole
2 spring onions, finely chopped
1 red apple, cored and sliced

1 green apple, cored and sliced
1/2 tsp nutmeg
1 tsp paprika pepper
140 ml/1/4pt stock
140 ml/1/4pt white wine
140 ml/1/4pt cider vinegar
salt and pepper

TO SERVE: 2 dsp parsley, finely chopped

Serves 6

Prick the sausages. Melt the butter and brown sugar in the pan and cook together until caramelised. Add the sausages and toss around for 3-4 minutes until golden. Add the onions, mushrooms, spring onions and apples and toss around. Next, in with the nutmeg, paprika pepper, stock, wine and cider vinegar. Simmer for 15-20 minutes. Garnish with finely chopped parsley.

A PEACH OF A JAM AND BREAD PUDDING

Bread filled with jam and cooked the French way in milk and egg, then fried in the pan, makes a very simple pudding if served with a little fruit salad.

4 baby brioche
4 dsp peach jam
3 peaches, chopped
280 ml/1/2pt milk or milk & cream mixed

1 tsp cinnamon powder
2 eggs, lightly beaten
30g/1oz butter
30g/1oz icing sugar

Fruit salad
3 peaches
1 passion fruit

1 star fruit

Serves 4

Cut the brioche into slices and spread with peach jam and chopped, tinned peaches. Sandwich together. Mix together the milk, 1/2 tsp cinnamon powder and beaten egg and dip the sandwiched bread into it. Drain off excess egg mixture, then fry in a pan with hot, melted butter until crispy and golden. Dust with icing sugar mixed with remainder of cinnamon powder. Drain on kitchen paper and serve with a simple fruit salad of peaches, star fruit and passion fruit.

Overleaf: a peach of a jam and bread pudding

LIGHTENING
LUNCHES

L unch is becoming more and more fashionable but today the emphasis is on food that is very quick to prepare.

Soup, crusty bread topped with vegetables, fish tart or a liquid lunch whizzed in a glass are only some of my speedy, healthy lunch ideas.

Lunch is that mid-day meal that everyone should enjoy, whether it is something you cook and eat alone or cater for the unexpected visitor who drops in.

A WARM SALAD OF OVEN TOASTED VEGETABLES WITH TOASTED GARLIC CRUMBS

I am always pleased to find a dish that is as popular with vegetarians as with those who enjoy a good fillet of steak. This dish can be made with a variety of vegetables and the crumbs of white or brown bread. Vegetables can vary with the season.

Garlic crumbs
6-8 slices wholemeal bread
2 cloves garlic
2 dsp olive oil

Oven roasted vegetables
1 red onion
1 yellow pepper
1 orange pepper
1 courgette

340g/12oz assorted mushroom
1 tsp honey
1 tsp olive oil
1 tsp balsamic vinegar

Serves 4

Cut the crusts from the bread, sprinkle with garlic and olive oil. Toast in the oven for 8-10 minutes until dry and crumbly. Blend the crumbs until crunchy. Be careful not to overblend. Wash, prepare and slice the vegetables. A sprinkling of honey, olive oil and balsamic vinegar will improve the flavour of the vegetables. Place in a foil lined baking sheet. Roast in the oven until cooked at 400°F/200°C/gas number 6 for approximately 15-20 minutes. Serve hot, layered with garlic crumbs and spoon over the roasted juices of honey, vinegar and oil.

HEALTHY LUNCH IN A GLASS

A very quick, healthy way to serve fruit or vegetable drinks at lunchtime which can be made in minutes in an electric blender or juicer.

High energy banana drink
2 bananas
1 tsp honey

1 tsp wheat germ oil
4 oranges, freshly squeezed

High fibre drink
1 cup grated celery
2 cups grated carrot

280ml/1/2pt apple juice
1 tsp chives

Serves 1

To make the banana drink, mush the bananas with the honey and wheat germ oil. Pour into a glass with freshly squeezed orange juice and serve. To make the high fibre drink, whizz all the ingredients together in a blender. Chill well and serve. Garnish with finely chopped chives.

BRUSCHETTA

This flavoured toasted bread is ideal to serve with many dishes. The toppings can vary from sun-dried tomato paste to pesto and tapenade. One of my favourites is the simplest of all, garlic and olive oil.

2-3 baguettes
olive oil, heated
2-3 cloves garlic, finely chopped

Alternatives
2 dsp pesto sauce
2 dsp sun-dried tomato paste
2 dsp tapenade

Serves 2

Slice the bread at an angle into pieces ½" thick. Pour over the heated olive oil and finely chopped garlic. Then toast under a pre-heated grill, until toasted and golden. If using an alternative topping, spread the paste over the top and grill as above. Serve hot or cold.

MONKFISH TART

For a lightning lunch, it is possible to make a pie or tart with fish, if you use filo pastry. This low fat pastry can be bought in sheets, already rolled out.

4-5 sheets of filo pastry
butter and egg to brush

Filling
450g/1lb monkfish tails
½ lemon juice and rind
1 dsp parsley, finely chopped
1 courgette, grated

4 eggs
140ml /¼pt yoghurt
2 dsp sun-dried tomatoes, chopped
100g/4oz mozzarella cheese

TO SERVE: 140ml/¼pt yoghurt, black pepper, 1 tsp pesto sauce

Serves 4

Brush the filo sheets with melted butter before layering in the flan dish. When the layers are pressed lightly in place, brush the top layer with beaten egg. Trim the membrane from the monkfish. Remove the centre, bone and cut the fish into small cubes. Sprinkle with lemon juice, rind and parsley. Peel and grate the courgette, and squeeze out any excess liquid. Beat the eggs lightly, add the yoghurt and mix. Assemble the pie together. Layer the fish into the filo pastry loose, add the courgette and sun-dried tomatoes with any excess liquid squeezed out and pour over the egg mixture. Sprinkle with mozzarella cheese, bake at 400°F/200°C/gas number 6 for 20-25 minutes. To serve, mix together ¼ pint yoghurt, black pepper and 1 tsp pesto sauce to make a dressing.

Overleaf: bruschetta and monkfish tart

CHICKEN CHARGRILLED WITH LEMON AND HERBS IN A MEDITERRANEAN SAUCE

Chicken fillets are invaluable when you need a quick meal. They defrost well in a microwave. If you don't have time to marinade, then chicken tossed in olive oil, lemon and herbs will improve the flavour.

3 chicken fillets
2 dsp olive oil
2 dsp lemon juice
1 dsp parsley, finely chopped
2 cloves garlic, finely chopped
4 spring onions, cut into 1" strips

1 tsp caster sugar
140ml/¼pt tomato juice
1 tsp sun-dried tomato paste
8-10 leaves basil, coarsely chopped
salt and pepper

Serves 3

Cut the chicken into ribbon strips, toss in 1 dsp oil, lemon juice and herbs and place on a hot oiled grill pan. Grill for 3-4 minutes on either side until well cooked. To make the sauce, heat the oil, add the garlic, spring onions, sugar to sweeten, tomato juice and paste, and simmer for 3-4 minutes. Add the grilled chicken pieces and heat thoroughly. Just before serving, add the coarsely shredded basil and seasoning.

BASIC FRENCH DRESSING

A basic French dressing can be served on its own or accompanied with many simple ingredients e.g. sun-dried tomatoes, diced smoked bacon or anchovies.

salt and pepper
¼ tsp dry mustard
1 dsp vinegar
3 dsp olive oil
55g/2oz diced, smoked bacon

Serves 4

Combine the salt, pepper and mustard. Add the vinegar and oil, and mix until emulsified. If the dressing is heated slightly, the flavour will be improved. Add the cooked, diced bacon before serving.

BLACKBERRY FLUMMERY

Flummeries, fools and sorbets are puddings packed full of fresh fruit with light, refreshing texture. I find that quick puddings like these are best made with seasonal berries and fruits full of flavour and goodness.

450g/1lb blackberries	15g/$\frac{1}{2}$oz demerara sugar
70ml/$\frac{1}{8}$pt water	pinch nutmeg

Egg custard	
280ml/$\frac{1}{2}$pt milk	15g/$\frac{1}{2}$oz caster sugar
3 egg yolks	few drops vanilla essence

Sauce	
140ml/$\frac{1}{4}$pt yoghurt, cream or fromage frais	55g/2oz hazelnuts

TO DECORATE: mint leaves, 1 dsp brown sugar

Serves 3-4

Wash and poach the blackberries in the water, sugar and nutmeg, then cool. Spoon $\frac{1}{3}$ mixture into the bottom of the dessert glasses and reserve 3 dsp of the purée for decoration. Heat the milk slightly. Add the whisked egg yolks, sugar and vanilla essence. Cook over a gentle heat until thickened but do not boil as the mixture will curdle. In a mixing bowl, gently fold the yoghurt and fruit purée into the cold custard. Fold to create a marbling effect, then fold in the hazelnuts and spoon on top of the berries. Decorate with a little purée, brown sugar, hazelnuts and mint.

A HOT BRAMLEY AND BRAMBLE PUDDING

It is hard to better our fresh, seasonal fruit if it's a quick, delicious, fast pudding you're looking for. This can be made in summer with strawberries, raspberries and currants or in autumn with Bramley apples, blackberries and plums flavoured with a hint of cinnamon.

2 Bramley or eating apples	170g/6oz mascarpone cheese
225g/$\frac{1}{2}$lb plums	225g/8oz yoghurt
225g/$\frac{1}{2}$lb blackberries	1 dsp lemon juice
70ml/$\frac{1}{8}$pt water	1 dsp brown sugar
30g/1oz demerara sugar	30g/1oz hazelnuts, chopped
pinch cinnamon	

Serves 6-8

Cut the apples into wedges. Stone and slice the plums. Wash the blackberries. Gently poach the fruit in water, demerara sugar and cinnamon until slightly softened approx. 3-4 minutes. Spoon onto the serving dish. Mix together the mascarpone and the yoghurt. Spoon over the fruit. Sprinkle with the lemon juice, brown sugar and nuts, and flash below a hot grill until bubbling and golden.

MEALS IN MINUTES

More and more often in this busy world we are looking for meals that are quick to prepare, easy to cook yet are healthy and packed full of goodness.

Today with a little extra care given to careful shopping and a few well-chosen jars and packets, you will be amazed at the way you can make a variety of meals in minutes.

A SPEEDY THAI CHICKEN CURRY

This is a mild tasting fragrant curry which is always popular with my family. Preparation requires little slicing or chopping. The Thai curry paste and can of coconut milk create the flavour.

450g/1lb chicken pieces
1 dsp honey
1 dsp olive oil
6-8 spring onions, chopped
2 cloves garlic, finely chopped

1 dsp green curry paste
1/2 lemon, juice only
pinch of salt
280 ml/1/2pt coconut milk
2 tsp basil, coarsely shredded

Serves 4

Toss the chicken pieces in honey, add to the hot oiled pan and cook for 5-6 minutes. The fine strips will ensure that the chicken cooks quickly. Toss often. Add the chopped spring onions and garlic, and cook for a further 2 minutes. Add the curry paste and lemon juice and cook for 2 minutes, to release the flavour and spices. Add a pinch of salt, coconut milk and coarsely shredded basil. Cook for a further 3-4 minutes, before serving.

FLAVOURSOME COCONUT RICE

It is easy to flavour rice, especially basmati, but patna long grain rice also works well. Freezer rice is excellent, if you are in a hurry, as it re-heats in the microwave in 3 minutes, or over hot water in 5-6 minutes.

450g/1lb rice
70 ml/1/8pt coconut milk

1 lemon, rind only
1 dsp parsley, finely chopped

Serves 4

Re-heat the freezer rice in a colander over a pan of boiling water, until hot and steaming. Sprinkle with coconut milk, lemon rind and parsley. Mix thoroughly, then serve.

THAI STIR-FRIED PRAWNS

One of the tastiest ways I know to cook prawns is in a stir-fry. This one is packed full of the aromatic flavours of ginger, garlic, lemon grass and chilli, then flavoured with soy and fish sauce.

2 cloves garlic
1 dsp oil
1" root ginger, chopped
1 red chilli, chopped
1 tsp chilli paste
1 tsp lemon grass paste

4 spring onions, chopped
225g/8oz oyster mushrooms
225g/8oz prawns, fresh or frozen
1 tsp soy sauce
1 dsp oyster sauce

TO SERVE parsley or coriander

Serves 2-3

Cook the garlic in the hot oil, then add ginger, chilli, chilli paste and lemon grass paste. Cook for 2 minutes. to release the flavours, then add the spring onions, mushrooms and prawns. Cook for a further 2 minutes. Finally add the soy sauce and oyster sauce and heat through. Garnish with parsley or coriander.

TOASTED PRAWNS WITH CHEESE

With a bag of prawns in the freezer, you are never stuck for a quick meal. This recipe combines defrosted prawns with melted cheese, bacon and spring onions to make a very tasty snack. Use bacon that is mild in flavour and cheese that melts beautifully e.g. gruyère or mozzarella.

30g/1oz butter
2 cloves garlic, chopped
2 spring onions, chopped
115g/4oz bacon, cut into strips

225g/8oz prawns
2 dsp lemon juice
pinch of salt
1/2 tsp cayenne pepper

Sauce
140 ml/1/4pt cream or yoghurt
55g/2oz mozzarella or gruyère cheese

Serves 3-4

Melt the butter in the pan, add the garlic, spring onions and bacon and cook for several minutes. Add the de-frosted prawns, sprinkle with the lemon juice, salt and cayenne pepper and cook for several minutes. To make the sauce, add the cream and cheese to the pan. Heat until melted, then flash below a very hot grill until bubbling and golden. Serve hot with wheaten triangles.

A PRAWN SALSA WITH A SPICY ORIENTAL DRESSING

Prawns are invaluable as they taste as good cold as hot. However, I find that they are equally good if combined with a spicy, oriental dressing. If possible, allow the prawns to marinate for 15 minutes before serving.

Oriental Dressing
1 tsp brown sugar
4 dsp oil
2 dsp red wine vinegar
1 tsp soy sauce

few drops Tabasco
1/2 tsp garlic
black pepper

115g/4oz prawns, defrosted
2 tomatoes, diced

small bunch of chives

TO SERVE salad leaves, finely mixed

Serves 2-4

To make the dressing, combine together the sugar, oil, vinegar, soy sauce, Tabasco, garlic and black pepper. Add the prawns, tomatoes and chives and toss lightly together. Leave to marinate for 15 minutes. Serve with salad leaves and finely chopped chives.

Overleaf: Thai stir-fried prawns, toasted prawns, prawn salsa

WONDERFUL WHITING
COOKED WITH RELISH

If it is a quick meal you're after, then I think you will find fish ideal as it cooks in minutes whether you are cooking, cod, haddock or whiting. This crusty, light topping of a tasty relish, combined with egg whites, gives a very different light fish dish, ideal served with pasta.

4 whiting fillets	pepper
2 dsp lemon juice	

Topping
70 ml/1/8pt mayonnaise	few drops Tabasco sauce
2 dsp relish, cucumber, onion or corn	2 egg whites, beaten
1 dsp parsley	

Serves 2-4

Layer the fish fillets in an oven-proof dish. Sprinkle with lemon juice and black pepper, bake in an oven at 400°F/200°C/gas number 6 for 12-15 minutes. To make the topping, mix together the mayonnaise, relish, parsley, Tabasco sauce and stiffly beaten egg whites. Spoon over the top of the fish and cook in the oven at 400°F/200°C/gas number 6 for 5-6 minutes.

MEAL IN A BOWL SOUP
MADE WITH GARDEN PEAS

There's nothing quite like the flavour of home-made soup and this one made with frozen peas is packed full of flavour and colour. If using bought stock cubes, then the addition of a dash of sherry and a pinch of sugar helps to disguise the saltiness of some stock cubes.

1 dsp oil	1.1L/2pt vegetable or chicken stock
1 large onion, diced	2 dsp parsley
900g/2lb frozen peas	1 dsp cream or yoghurt
2 spring onions, finely chopped	

Serves 6

Heat the oil, add the diced onion and cook over a gentle heat for 6-7 minutes. Add the peas, spring onions, stock, bring to the boil and simmer for no longer than 6 minutes or the colour will spoil. Add the parsley, cool a little, then liquidise or blend the soup until smooth. Return to the pot, re-heat, add a little cream or yoghurt just before serving. Serve with tomato bruschettas.

SPICED GRAPEFRUIT

Use either fresh or tinned grapefruit for this recipe. I prefer the flavour of fresh grapefruit but it takes time to segment properly.

2 grapefruit
30g/1oz demerara sugar
1/4tsp cinnamon powder

Serves 4

Place the grapefruit segments in an oven-proof dish. Sprinkle with demerara sugar and a hint of cinnamon. Cook below a very hot grill until hot and blackened.

PASTA PAPARADELLE

Pasta, whether fresh or dried, is so easy to cook. Just perfect with this fish dish.

225g/8oz dried pasta
2.25L/3-4pt water
pinch of salt

1 dsp oil
1 dsp chives, finely chopped

Serves 4

Cook the dried pasta in boiling, salted water and oil for 6 minutes until cooked *al dente*. Drain. While still hot, sprinkle with 1 dsp oil and chives, then serve.

OLD-FASHIONED HONEY-BAKED APPLES WITH BLACKBERRIES AND PLUMS

Autumn fruit bakes in the oven very quickly. Fill the apples with fruit, nuts and honey, then bake.

3 apples
1 plum

55g/2oz blackberries
2 dsp honey

Serves 3

Core the apples and pack with diced plum and chopped blackberries. Pour over with honey and bake in the oven at 400°F/200°C/gas number 6 for approximately 15-20 minutes until the apple softens. Serve hot with lemon sorbet.

A HONEYED CHICKEN AND WHOLEGRAIN CASSEROLE with COUS COUS TOPPING

When speed is of the essence, chicken casserole is ideal. This tasty casserole has a nutty cous cous topping. As an alternative, make the topping with brown or white breadcrumbs.

1 tsp olive oil
30g/1oz polyunsaturated fat
1 onion, finely chopped
680g/1 ½lb chicken fillets, cut into strips

70ml/⅛ pt vegetable or chicken stock
1 tsp wholegrain mustard
70ml/⅛ pt honey, liquid

Caramelised Apples and Celery
Hint of olive oil
1 red apple, unpeeled and cut into wedges
1 green apple, unpeeled and cut into wedges

2 sticks celery, cut into ribbon matchsticks
1 tsp demerara sugar

Nutty Cous Cous Topping
15g/½oz polyunsaturated fat
55g/2oz pine nuts or hazelnuts
2 dsp parsley, finely chopped

170g/6oz cous cous, steeped in
280ml/½ pt chicken stock

Serves 6-8

Heat oil and polyunsaturated fat together on a non stick pan, add chopped onion and cook for 2-3 minutes until opaque, softened and lightly browned. Add chicken strips and cook over a high temperature for approximately 8 minutes, until the chicken is crispy and golden. Add stock, mustard and honey to chicken and mix together. Simmer for 2-3 minutes, until sauce has thickened slightly. Pour all of the chicken and sauce into an ovenproof casserole. Add olive oil, apple slices and celery to the pan and cook together with any remaining chicken and honey juices left on the base of the pan. Add the demerara sugar and cook for 2 minutes, then pour over the top of the chicken in the ovenproof casserole. To make the topping, add the polyunsaturated fat, nuts and parsley to the hot pan and toss around for 1 minute. Add the cous cous which has absorbed all the water. Toss around until well mixed, then pour over the apples, celery and chicken. Smooth on top and bake in the oven at 375°F/190°C/gas number 5 for approximately 25 minutes, until topping is crunchy and golden.

COUNTRY CHICKEN PATE

This is a cold, chunky pâté which is ideal for lunch or served as a starter. The basic recipe can be made in individual ramekins or doubled in quantity and adapted to be served in a large dish. Whether you are catering for a small or large number, add dissolved gelatine to the mixture for a firmer pâté.

Basic Mixture
450g/1lb chicken fillets, diced and steamed
1 tbsp lemon juice
1 tsp fresh coriander, chopped

Sauce
115g/4oz mayonnaise
115g/4oz yoghurt (Greek or low fat)
55g/2oz Mascarpone cheese
½ tsp paprika pepper

30g/1oz roasted hazelnuts, chopped
salt and pepper
1 spring onion, finely chopped

Serves 3

Large Terrine Pâté
Double quantity of above basic mixture
1 tsp lemon juice
2 apples, chopped
1 pear, chopped (optional)

4 stalks celery, finely chopped
15g/½oz gelatine, dissolved
(optional)

Serves 6-8

Dice chicken fillets and steam over a pan of boiling water until cooked, approximately 8-10 minutes. Cooking time will depend on the size of chicken diced pieces. When cooked and still warm, sprinkle chicken with lemon juice and coriander. Toss around and leave to cool. To make the sauce, mix together mayonnaise, yoghurt and Mascarpone cheese until smooth and creamy. Add paprika pepper, hazelnuts, salt, pepper and spring onion. Mix together, then transfer to lightly oiled ramekins and chill in the refrigerator for at least 1 hour. Unmould and serve. To make a large pâté, double the quantity of basic quantity and prepare in the same way. Toss apples and pear in lemon juice to prevent browning. Add celery, apples, pear and gelatine to the mixture. Gelatine will give the pâté a better set and make slicing easier. Mix together and transfer to a terrine or loaf tin lined with oiled cling film. Chill in the refrigerator until firm and well set. Unmould and serve with salad.

SUPPER IN A SECOND

I f you live in the country as I do, you probably remember how supper used to be. A cup of tea with a sandwich, a bun or a slice of cake was the order of the day.

Today, the idea of supper has changed. It is now a one-course dish that can be prepared, cooked and served in no time at all. Often it is a savoury dish with toppings which can be served with salad, salsa, pasta or quickly baked potatoes.

SEA FOOD PASTA WITH MUSSELS

If it is a quick supper you are making, then sea food and pasta are ideal. If making mussels, make sure they are tightly closed before cooking and if they haven't opened up after cooking, discard them.

450g/1lb mussels
570 ml/1pt cold water
1 dsp olive oil
few stalks parsley
1/2 onion, cut into chunks
140 ml/1/4pt dry white wine

garlic
2-3 spring onions
3 leeks
170g/6oz pasta shells
140 ml/1/4pt cream
2 cloves parsley

Serves 2-3

Scrub and wash the mussels. Bring the water, wine, parsley and onion to the boil. Add the mussels and cook for 6-7 minutes. Heat the oil and cook the garlic. Add the spring onions and leeks and cook for 2-3 minutes. Reduce the strained stock in which the mussels were cooked to 1/3 pint for the sauce. Add the stock to the cooked vegetables, the mussels, cooked pasta shells, cream and parsley. Heat thoroughly and serve with crusty bread.

SPAGHETTI WITH TURKEY AND BOLOGNESE SAUCE

I find when I am cooking for the family, mince is just ideal and isn't it great to find a variety such as turkey? This one is low in fat, easily digested and quick to cook. I find that turkey mince needs extra flavour added before cooking e.g. balsamic vinegar and Worcestershire sauce.

2.25L/4pt water
1 dsp olive oil
1/2 tsp salt
450g/1lb spaghetti
450g/1lb turkey mince
2 dsp balsamic vinegar
1 tsp Worcestershire sauce
2 dsp parsley

salt and pepper
1 dsp oil
1 onion
garlic
2 tsp chilli paste
2 tbsp sun-dried tomato paste
280 ml/1/2pt vegetable stock

TO SERVE: parsley

Serves 6-8

Bring the water to the boil, add the olive oil and salt, then the spaghetti and cook for 8-9 minutes until tender but al dente. Then drain and keep warm. Place the mince in a large bowl and toss in the balsamic vinegar, Worcestershire sauce, parsley and seasoning. Cook the oil, onion and garlic for just a couple of minutes, then add the turkey mince. Cook over a high heat for several minutes, then reduce the temperature and continue to cook for a further 8-10 minutes. Add the chilli paste, tomato paste and stock. Heat thoroughly and serve with the parsley.

FRESH TAGLIATELLE WITH A TRIO OF MUSHROOMS

A vegetarian idea with pasta made with mushrooms in a cream or yoghurt sauce. Fresh pasta is now widely available and cooks quickly. However, dried pasta is a very convenient food to have stacked away in a food cupboard and cooks in 5-6 minutes.

450g/1lb fresh pasta	1 dsp olive oil
2.25 L/4pt boiling water	1/2 tsp salt

1 dsp olive oil	3-4 spring onions, cut into chunks
15g/1/2oz polyunsaturated fat	450g/1lb mushrooms, assorted
1" root ginger	

2 dsp yoghurt or cream
2 dsp crème fraîche

TO SERVE: 1 dsp parsley, finely chopped

Serves 4

Place the pasta in a pot of oiled, salted, boiling water and cook rapidly for 3 minutes. Drain and toss in a little olive oil before serving. Heat the oil and fat in a pan, add the ginger and spring onions and cook for 2 minutes. Add the mushrooms and cook for a further 2 minutes until cooked. Add the yoghurt and crème fraîche. Garnish with the parsley and serve.

Overleaf: fresh tagliatelle and mushrooms

A SUPER SUPPER FISH PIE

A good fish pie is hard to beat if made with un-dyed, smoked fish, a really tasty sauce and a crunchy topping. This sauce is made with the two cheeses, mozzarella and cheddar, which give texture, flavour and colour.

680g/1 ½lb fish, smoked or unsmoked	black pepper
280 ml/½pt milk	2 tsp lemon juice

Sauce
280ml/½pt strained milk, from fish cooking liquid	55g/2oz mozzarella cheese
280ml/½pt milk	55g/2oz cheddar cheese
30g/1oz butter	1 dsp parsley
45g/1 ½oz plain flour	

Topping
1 dsp spring onions, finely chopped	225g/8oz matzo meal or wholemeal flour
30g/1oz polyunsaturated fat	1 egg

TO SERVE:
450g/1lb cooked beetroot	1 dsp balsamic vinegar
1 red onion	dash Tabasco
1 dsp olive oil	salt and pepper

Serves 4-6

Skin the fish and poach in the milk, black pepper and a hint of lemon juice for 5 minutes. Strain the milk into a jug from the cooked fish. Heat together the strained milk, the remaining ½ pint milk, butter, flour and cheeses. Bring to the boil and cook for 30 seconds. Sprinkle a little parsley over the fish before pouring over the sauce. Cook the spring onions in the butter, add the meal and egg and continue cooking until the mixture resembles a crumbly topping. Sprinkle over the fish pie and bake in the oven at 375°F/190°C/gas number 5 for 20-25 minutes. Serve with cooked beetroot tossed with cooked and raw red onions, 1 dsp balsamic vinegar, a dash of Tabasco sauce and salt and pepper.

A HONEYED SULTANA-TOPPED APPLE SAUCE CAKE

Here is an apple sauce cake that you can serve as a pudding or if you just fancy a cup of tea and a slice of cake, then this one is just as good. The cinnamon and honeyed sultana topping is delicious, especially if served with yoghurt or fresh cream.

1 Bramley apple	170g/6oz caster sugar
1 dsp water	55g/2oz sultanas
15g/½oz sugar	2 small eggs, lightly beaten
1/4 tsp cinnamon powder	170g/6oz self-raising flour
115g/4oz butter	

Topping
55g/2oz sultanas
1/2 tsp cinnamon powder
2 dsp honey

Serves 8-10

Peel, core and slice the apple, then poach in the water, sugar and cinnamon powder for 3-4 minutes until cooked and soft. Leave to cool. Cream together the butter and sugar until light and fluffy. Add the cold, puréed apple, sultanas and lightly beaten egg. Mix well together, then add the sieved flour in 2-3 additions. Mix well, then transfer to an oiled and lined loose-bottomed tin. Cook at 375°F/190°C/gas number 5 for 30 minutes until golden and firm to the touch. Unmould. Bubble together the sultanas, cinnamon and honey and pour over the top of the cake when still warm.

AN ALMOND AND RASPBERRY TART

Here's a speedy tart which does not require making or rolling out of pastry. It makes a perfect end to any supper.

Almond biscuit base
45g/1/2oz butter
1 dsp honey
170g/6oz amaretto biscuits
1 egg yolk

450g/1lb fresh raspberries
30g/1oz demerara sugar
1/2 tsp cinnamon powder

Topping
340g/12oz Greek yoghurt
55g/2oz demerara sugar

Serves 8-10

Melt the butter, add the honey and biscuits and stir until well coated. Transfer to a loose bottomed flan dish, 7-8" in diameter, press down well. Brush with lightly beaten egg and flash below a hot grill for 30 seconds to cook the egg and seal the base. This will stop the juice of the raspberries from leaking through the base. Top with raspberries and sprinkle with demerara sugar and cinnamon powder. Spoon the yoghurt over the berries, dust with demerara sugar and flash below a very hot grill until bubbling and golden (2 minutes). Chill in the fridge before serving.

DINNER IN A
DASH

Few people have time today to organise, prepare and cook for dinner parties, except on special occasions.

I find that we prefer food that is quick to prepare and cook. The choice of food includes pasta, sauces and pesto to help you on your way with quick coatings.

Puddings come together in minutes with a pinch of imagination and a few ingredients to hand.

A GARDEN FRESH ASPARAGUS SOUP

When you are in a hurry, I find a simple, yet elegant soup is hard to better. The flavour of asparagus is so good and it is quick to prepare and cook. The only preparation of asparagus is washing; I find the spears, finely sliced, make an attractive garnish.

450g/1lb fresh asparagus
2 dsp olive oil
1 leek, finely chopped
1 onion, finely chopped
2 spring onions

1 potato, diced
1.1L/2pt chicken stock
1 tsp parsley
salt and pepper

TO SERVE: 2-3 asparagus spears, cooked; 1 dsp finely chopped parsley

Serves 4-6

Wash, trim and chop the asparagus into 1" pieces. Heat the oil, then add the chopped leek, onion and spring onion. Add the peeled and finely diced potato, then cook over a low heat for 10-12 minutes to cook the vegetables and release the strength of the onions. The potato will help thicken the soup. Add the chopped asparagus, stock, parsley and seasoning and simmer for approximately 10 minutes until tender. Blend, then serve hot topped with blanched asparagus spears and a little finely chopped parsley.

SEARED TUNA STEAK

Fish is ideal if you are looking for food that cooks quickly and if you are looking for something that is unusual, then try fresh tuna, totally different in flavour and texture from tuna in a can. Tuna is also a fish which is easy to cook as it holds its shape. Tuna resembles fillet steak in colour and texture when at its freshest. Tuna needs a sauce. This light, spicy, creamy sauce complements tuna.

2 tuna steaks, 115-170g/4-6oz each
salt
2 dsp lime juice
15g/¹/₂oz butter
1 dsp oil

1 dsp peppercorns, crushed
1 dsp chives, finely chopped
2 dsp cream
2 tsp lemon juice

Serves 2

Sprinkle the fish with salt and lime juice. Melt the butter in a frying pan, add the oil and cook the fish for several minutes on either side. Add the peppercorns, chives, cream and lemon juice and heat thoroughly until the sauce thickens. Then serve. With any fish, be careful not to over-cook as it will fall apart very easily.

PILAFF WITH HERBS AND SPICES

Pilaff is good to serve with an Italian lamb dish and here is one that echoes to the flavours of the crust. This is a spicy, herb one which is delicious with the hint of colour from the red onions and perfume from the crushed coriander seeds.

1 dsp oil
1 red onion
340g/12oz patna rice
570 ml/1pt vegetable stock
salt and pepper

1 tsp thyme, chopped
1 dsp parsley, chopped
1/2 tsp coriander seeds, crushed
55g/2oz pine nuts or hazelnuts

TO SERVE: 2 dsp parsley, finely chopped

Serves 4

Heat the oil and gently fry the red onion for 2-3 minutes until softened. Add the rice and stir until shiny and glistening. Add the stock and seasoning and simmer for approximately 8 minutes until the grains are tender and the liquid absorbed. Add the thyme, parsley, crushed coriander seeds and pine nuts. Heat thoroughly. Be careful not to overcook, and serve at once. Garnish with parsley.

AN ITALIAN RACK OF LAMB

A roast rack of lamb is the ideal choice for a dinner. It cooks quickly, looks delicious and tastes superb especially if you give it the Italian treatment; that is topped and crusted with black olives and herbs, then roasted in the oven until cooked and crusted on the outside. I like to serve this with rice or a pilaff and a roasted redcurrant sauce.

1 rack lamb, 8-9 cutlets
2 dsp black olive paste

Crust
55g/2oz white breadcrumbs
1 dsp thyme, chopped or dried
1 dsp mint, chopped

1 tsp coriander seeds, crushed
salt and pepper
2 dsp olive oil

Serves 4

Prepare the lamb by removing the layer of fat and scrape the bones, leaving 2" of the bone bare of fat. Cover the skin side of the rack of lamb with olive paste and pat down firmly. Make the crust by mixing together the breadcrumbs, thyme, mint, coriander seeds, salt, pepper and olive oil to mix to a paste. Pat over the olive paste, sprinkle with oil and cook in a pre-heated oven at 400°F/200°C/gas number 7 for 30-40 minutes if you like lamb a little pink. If you like your lamb well cooked, slightly longer. Roasting is a delicious way to cook this rack of lamb.

A ROASTED REDCURRANT SAUCE

A tasty, colourful sauce to serve with lamb. I like to make the sauce in a roasting dish with the best of the flavour from the roasting juices. However, for a more attractive sauce, strain the juices first.

140 ml/1/4pt strained lamb juices
dash red wine
1 tsp olive paste

1 dsp redcurrant jelly
1 tsp thyme, chopped

Overleaf· pilaff with herbs and spices, an Italian rack of lamb

Serves 4

Strain the meat juices from the roasting dish, then add the wine, olive paste and redcurrant jelly. Bring to the boil, whisking all the time, then add the chopped thyme and serve at once.

A HOT SALAD OF SPINACH WITH PARMESAN AND GARLIC

A robust way to cook and serve spinach. This tasty warm salad dish is perfect to serve with fish, lamb or chicken.

450g/1lb fresh spinach leaves	*2 cloves garlic, chopped*
1 dsp olive oil	*55g/2oz parmesan cheese*

Serves 4

Wash the spinach leaves, then pat dry. Heat the oil and garlic in a pan until golden. Add the washed spinach and cook for 1-2 minutes tossing all the time. Sprinkle with shaved parmesan cheese, then serve at once.

EASTERN FLAVOURED CHICKEN DISH WITH LEMON GRASS FLAVOURED RICE

With the vast array of exotic flavours that we can lay our hands on today, it's not difficult to take plain chicken fillets and turn them into a dish you would not be ashamed to serve to your friends for dinner. This dish is light, aromatic and perfumed.

680g/1 ½lb chicken fillets

Marinade	
2 chillies red or green, diced	*1 dsp curry paste*
1″ root ginger	*2 dsp olive oil*
1 lime, juice only	*few drops soy sauce*
2 cloves garlic	

1 dsp olive oil	*280 ml/½pt coconut milk*
1 onion	*1 mango or peach, sliced*
2 spring onions	*1 dsp parsley, chopped*
280 ml/½pt vegetable stock	

Serves 4-6

Trim fat off the chicken and cut into ribbon strips. Into a blender add the chillies, ginger, lime juice, garlic, curry paste, olive oil, soy sauce and blend together before pouring over the chicken fillets and leave to marinade for 30 minutes in a covered dish. Heat the oil in a wok or large frying pan, then cook the onion and spring onion until crispy yet crunchy. Add the marinaded chicken a little at a time and cook for 5-6 minutes i.e. until light and tender. Add the stock and coconut milk and cook for 2-3 minutes. The coconut milk will thicken this sauce. Finally, add a sliced mango or peach. Heat thoroughly and serve garnished with parsley. Serve with basmati rice cooked with 2 stalks of lemon grass for flavour. Cook in the usual way, but be careful not to stir the rice or it will become sticky.

A BROKEN MERINGUE PUDDING
WITH A HOT PLUM SAUCE

Here's a great pudding that looks stunning and tastes delicious. It is made with meringues and a tin of plums, combined with yoghurt and crème fraîche or fromage frais. If liked, you can add a hint of cardamon – a tasty, perfumed pod/spice packed with flavours – or cinnamon which is more readily available.

2 pkt meringues, approximately 8-10 nests
280 ml/½pt Greek yoghurt
70-140 ml/⅛-¼pt crème fraîche or fromage frais
1x 340g/12oz can plums
½ tsp cinnamon or cardamon seeds, crushed

Serves 3-4

Crumble the meringues into a bowl, add the yoghurt and crème fraîche mixed together. Lightly toss, then spoon onto a serving bowl. Be careful not to over-mix or the volume will reduce considerably. Take the stones out of the plums and bubble with the cardamon or cinnamon for 1-2 minutes. Blend or sieve and when cool spoon over the crushed meringues, then serve. It is better to allow the sauce to cool, otherwise the yoghurt will become very soft and spoil the pudding.

ROASTED PEACHES WITH A
REDCURRANT SAUCE SERVED WITH
AMARETTO BISCUIT ICE CREAM

With a couple of cans of peaches and a tub of ice cream, you can easily make a stunning pudding. These peaches are grilled for several minutes until bubbling, crispy and golden and the ice cream is simply put together with a hint of liqueur mixed with vanilla ice cream.

2 cans peach halves, 12 approximately
2 dsp redcurrant jelly
55g/2oz demerara sugar
1 tsp cinnamon powder

450g/1lb tub vanilla ice cream
55g/2oz crumbled amaretto biscuits
dash of amaretto liqueur

Serves 4-6

Arrange the peaches on an ovenproof dish. Top with softened redcurrant jelly, then sprinkle with demerara sugar and cinnamon mixed together. Flash below a very hot grill until bubbling and golden for approximately 2 minutes. Mix the ice cream with the biscuits and liqueur, then return to the freezer to harden before serving.

Overleaf: a broken meringue pudding with a hot plum sauce, roasted peaches with a redcurrant sauce

SIMPLY
CHRISTMAS

———◆❈◆———

Do you find that Christmas lunch is the one meal that allows you to escape to your childhood and enjoy again the traditional flavours of this very special time?

There are many demands which fall on the cook at this time of year. Old favourites such as turkey and Christmas pudding reappear on the menu year after year. Take these favourites, give them each a different treatment and flavour for a quicker and more efficient way of cooking.

CRANBERRY AND ORANGE SAUCE

If it's a simple sauce you fancy, then a cranberry and orange one is hard to better. This sauce is sweetened and thickened with redcurrant jelly, which also keeps the colour bright red.

450g/1lb cranberries
140 ml/¼pt orange juice
55g/2oz caster sugar

2 dsp redcurrant jelly
½ orange, peel shredded

Serves 8-10

Wash the cranberries and poach in the pot with the orange juice and sugar for 6-7 minutes until they pop and start to soften. Add the redcurrant jelly to thicken the sauce and the orange rind to garnish. Serve hot or cold.

GINGER GLAZED CARROTS

Add ginger and honey to the traditional carrots to enhance the flavour.

900g/2lb carrots, lightly steamed wedges
30g/1oz butter
1" root ginger

2 dsp honey
1 dsp parsley

Serves 6

Steam the carrots for 10-12 minutes until cooked but still firm. In a separate pan, cook together the butter and ginger until just bubbling. Add the honey, carrots and parsley. Heat thoroughly and serve.

ROASTED ALL-SPICE POTATOES

There are as many ways to roast potatoes as there are to cook the turkey, whether you are roasting them around the turkey, or simply roasting them on their own in the oven.

6 potatoes, lightly steamed
2 tbsp balsamic vinegar
2 tbsp olive oil

2 tbsp honey
salt and pepper
½ tsp crushed all-spice

Serves 6

Steam the potatoes for 5-6 minutes then criss cross on top with a sharp knife. Place on a roasting dish and sprinkle with vinegar, oil, honey, seasoning and all-spice. Roast in the oven at 425°F/220°C/gas number 7 for 30 minutes, until crispy, golden and soft.

BUTTERED BRUSSELS SPROUTS

The secret in the cooking of Brussels sprouts is not to over-cook them. I find the microwave is an ideal way to cook them as they keep their colour.

70ml/⅛pt water
450g/1lb Brussels sprouts

30g/1oz butter, melted
30g/1oz hazelnuts, toasted

Serves 4-6

Cook the peeled sprouts in water in the microwave at low temperature for 3 minutes. Drain and pour into a serving dish. Pour over the hot butter and hazelnuts.

A CHRISTMAS HAM WITH
A KUMQUAT GLAZE

A ham well cooked can be just as much part of the Christmas tradition as the turkey. I find steeping the ham in cold water for up to 24 hours helps to remove the excess saltiness. Do remember to change the water several times during steeping. The kumquats give a most attractive look to the Christmas ham.

3-3.5kg/7-8lb ham
3.4 - 4.5L/6-8pt water
1 onion
1 leek
2 carrots
bunch herbs

6-8 cloves
450g/1lb kumquats, sliced
55g/2oz brown sugar
½ jar honey
6 cloves

Serves 10-12

Steep the ham in cold water for up to 24 hours. Remove. Fill a saucepan with fresh water and place ham in saucepan. Cook along with the onion, leeks, carrot, herbs and cloves. Bring to the boil and simmer gently for 1 hour. After this time, turn off the heat and leave the ham cooling in the water. Bubble the kumquats, 1 tsp brown sugar and honey together in the water for 3 minutes. When almost cool, remove the ham from the water. Peel the rind from the ham using a sharp knife and criss cross sharp slices across the layer of fat on the ham, then pour over the kumquat and honey glaze. Lift out the kumquats before pouring over the glaze. Then use whole cloves to stud the kumquats to the ham. Sprinkle with remainder of brown sugar and bake in the oven at 375°F/190°C/gas number 5 for 45 minutes - 1 hour or until cooked golden and glazed. Baste occasionally during cooking. Serve hot or cold.

Overleaf: Christmas ham, buttered Brussels sprouts, roasted all-spice potatoes

A CHRISTMAS SOUP

For Christmas lunch, a light, easy-to-make soup is just what is needed and I think you will find none better than the flavour of juniper or cinnamon, pears and a hint of parsnip combined and blended together.

450g/1lb parsnips or celeriac
450g/1lb pears

Vegetable stock
3.4 L/6pt water
1 onion, cut into chunks
1 leek
3 stalks celery

few black peppercorns
10 juniper berries, crushed
1/4 tsp cinnamon powder
salt and pepper

6 juniper berries, crushed or 1/2 tsp cinnamon powder
140 ml/1/4pt cream, whipped

Serves 8

Peel and chop the parsnips or celeriac. Peel the pears and cut into chunks but reserve the peel for the stock. Make the stock by boiling the water, onion, leek, celery, peppercorns, juniper berries, peel from pear, cinnamon and salt and pepper gently together for at least 1 hour. Strain as soon as possible and use, preferably the day it is made, or the stock will lose its strength of flavour. If storing overnight, keep in the 'fridge. Add half to the pot along with the parsnips or celeriac and pears, then simmer gently for 15-20 minutes until soft. Purée the soup in a blender until soft, then return to the pan with the remainder of the stock and re-heat together until the consistency of the soup is correct. Add the crushed juniper berries or cinnamon powder and re-heat with a little cream. Serve hot with a swirl of cream and crushed juniper berries or cinnamon powder on top.

CHRISTMAS ROASTED TURKEY

Christmas wouldn't be Christmas without a turkey and I find that every year I am looking for a new treatment and flavour. This year it is simplicity, with a traditional Irish stuffing and the best of simple, everyday vegetables treated with the spice and magic of Christmas. The decision to have a fresh or frozen turkey is a matter of choice. Remember to defrost thoroughly if using a frozen bird.

1x 4-4.5kg/9-10lb turkey, fresh or de-frosted

Traditional Irish stuffing
30g/1oz butter
1 onion, chopped
115g/4oz sausage meat
225g/8oz white breadcrumbs

1 lemon, rind only
4 dsp parsley, finely chopped
1 egg, lightly beaten
salt and pepper

To cook
55g/2oz butter, melted
6-8 rashers bacon

280 ml/1/2pt stock
1 dsp honey

Serves 8-10

Melt the butter in a frying pan, then lightly fry the onion and sausage meat until opaque and cooked. Add to the breadcrumbs along with the lemon rind, parsley, lightly beaten egg and seasoning. Mix well, then use to stuff the neck of the bird but never the cavity. Fold over the flap and transfer to a foil lined dish. Brush the entire turkey with melted butter, layer with strips of bacon and after setting on the foil, pour over the stock. Cook in the oven at 425°F/220°C/gas number 7 for 30 minutes and at 375°F/190°C/gas number 5 for 3 hours. Finally, turn heat up again to 425°F/220°C/gas number 7 open the foil, remove the bacon, brush with melted butter and honey and return to the heat to finally crisp up and become golden. Do not forget to allow the turkey to stand for 20 minutes before serving and carving. Serve with all the trimmings.

CHRISTMAS PUDDING

Here's a light, moist Christmas pudding that can be prepared in advance but cooked just minutes before you want to eat it. It is ideal for the microwave – hence the high quantity of raising agent. However, if you prefer to steam this one by the traditional method, then leave out 1 tsp baking powder, cover with greased, waxed paper and string, then steam for 2½ hours. This pudding will keep for several weeks if cooked this way.

225g/8oz mincemeat
170g/6oz sultanas
55g/2oz glacé cherries
1 tsp mixed spice
115g/4oz butter

115g/4oz soft brown sugar
3 small eggs
140g/5oz self-raising flour
30g/1oz ground almonds
1 tsp baking powder

Serves 8

Mix together the mincemeat, sultanas, cherries, spice and toss around for a few minutes. In a separate bowl, cream together the butter and sugar until light and creamy, then add the eggs, flour, ground almonds and baking powder in one addition. Mix well then add the fruit and fold in well before transferring to a well greased Pyrex bowl. If cooking in the microwave, cook at high temperature for 5 minutes plus 2 minutes standing time. If steaming by the traditional method, steam for 2½ hours. Serve hot with brandy sauce.

MY MUM'S BRANDY SAUCE

I have tasted many a brandy sauce and I reckon you will have bother trying to better this one. Adjust the quantity of brandy to suit your taste.

115g/4oz butter
115g/4oz soft brown sugar
70ml/⅛ pint brandy

1 egg yolk, lightly beaten
280ml/½ pint whipping cream
55g/2oz Brazil nuts, chopped

Serves 6

Melt the butter and sugar together and stir over a low heat until golden and the sugar has dissolved. Allow to cool slightly before adding the brandy and lightly beaten egg yolk. Mix well before adding the lightly whipped cream and Brazil nuts. Serve warm.

CHRISTMAS PEARS
WITH A WATERCRESS CREAM

An idea for a cold starter which can be made in advance. The conference pear is ideal for this dish as it poaches well and will retain its shape, provided you do not over-cook it.

4 pears
2.25L/4pt water
2 dsp caster sugar
pinch nutmeg

1 dsp lemon juice
450g/1lb pkt watercress
140 ml/¼ pt cream
115g/4 oz cream cheese e.g. Philadelphia

TO DECORATE: 30g/1oz nuts, chopped

Serves 4

Peel and core the pears from underneath, then poach in water, sugar, nutmeg and lemon juice for 3-4 minutes until just lightly softened. Remove from the pot and leave to cool. Cook the watercress in boiling water for 2 minutes. Strain the watercress then add to a blender with the cream and whizz to form a sauce. Use 2 dsp of the sauce to mix with the cheese. Transfer to a piping bag and fill the cavities of the cooled pears. Serve on a plate with a little of the watercress sauce spooned around the outside of the pears. Decorate with chopped nuts.

Index

Index

Index